Impossible Exchange

Impossible Exchange

Jean Baudrillard

Translated by Chris Turner

VERSO
London • New York

This edition first published by Verso 2001
© Verso 2001
Translation © Chris Turner 2001
First published as *L'Echange impossible*
© Editions Galilée 1999
All rights reserved

Verso
UK: 6 Meard Street, London W1F 0EG
USA:180 Varick Street, New York, NY 10014–4606
www.versobooks.com

Verso is the imprint of New Left Books

ISBN 1–85984–647–5
ISBN 1–85984–349–2 (pbk)

British Library Cataloguing in Publication Data
A catalogue record for this book is available from the
British Library

Library of Congress Cataloging-in-Publication Data

Baudrillard, Jean
        [Echange impossible. English]
        Impossible Exchange/Jean Baudrillard: translated by Chris Turner.
            p.   cm.
        ISBN 1–85984–647–5   ISBN 1–85984–349–2 (alk. paper)
        1. Reality. I. Title.

    B2430.B33973 E2513 2001
    194—dc21

                                                                            2001045420

Typeset by M Rules
Printed and bound in Great Britain by
The Bath Press, Avon

Contents

CONTENTS

The Flow of Change. The Cycle of Becoming. The Divide of Destiny

Poetic Transference

Translator's Foreword

I would like to thank Marie-Dominique Maison, Leslie Hill and Mike Gane for their help, direct and indirect, with the preparation of this translation.

There are no footnotes in the original French edition. All notes here are my own, and are intended to provide background information which an ordinary French reader (the woman on the metro to Denfert-Rochereau, perhaps) might be assumed to possess.

C.T.

Impossible Exchange

Impossible Exchange

Everything starts from impossible exchange. The uncertainty of the world lies in the fact that it has no equivalent anywhere; it cannot be exchanged for anything. The uncertainty of thought lies in the fact that it cannot be exchanged either for truth or for reality. Is it thought which tips the world over into uncertainty, or the other way round? This in itself is part of the uncertainty.

There is no equivalent of the world. That might even be said to be its definition – or lack of it. No equivalent, no double, no representation, no mirror. Any mirror whatsoever would still be part of the world. There is not enough room both for the world and for its double. So there can be no verifying of the world. This is, indeed, why 'reality' is an imposture. Being without possible verification, the world is a fundamental illusion. Whatever can be verified locally, the uncertainty of the world, taken overall, is not open to debate. There is no integral calculus of the universe. A differential calculus, perhaps? 'The Universe, made up of multiple sets, is not itself a set' (Denis Guedj).

This is how it is with any system. The economic sphere, the sphere of all exchange, taken overall, cannot be exchanged for anything. There is no meta-economic equivalent of the economy anywhere, nothing to exchange it for as such, nothing with which to redeem it in another world. It is, in a sense, insolvent, and in any event insoluble to a global intelligence. And so it, too, is of the order of a fundamental uncertainty.

This it tries to ignore. But the indeterminacy induces a fluctuation of equations and postulates at the very heart of the economic sphere and leads, in the end, to that sphere lurching off into speculation, its criteria and elements all interacting madly.

The other spheres – politics, law and aesthetics – are characterized by this same non-equivalence, and hence the same eccentricity. Literally, they have no meaning outside themselves and cannot be exchanged for anything. Politics is laden with signs and meanings, but seen from the outside it has none. It has nothing to justify it at a universal level (all attempts to ground politics at a metaphysical or philosophical level have failed). It absorbs everything which comes into its ambit and converts it into its own substance, but it is not able to convert itself into – or be reflected in – a higher reality which would give it a meaning.

Here again, this impossible equivalence finds expression in the increasing undecidability of its categories, discourses, strategies and issues. The political – together with its *mise-en-scène* and its discourse – proliferates in scale with its fundamental illusoriness.

There is great uncertainty, even in the sphere of living matter and biology. Schemes for genetic experimentation and investigation are becoming infinitely ramified, and the more ramified they become, the more the crucial question is left unanswered: who rules over life, who rules over death? Complex as it may be, the phenomenon of life cannot be exchanged for any ultimate purpose. One cannot conceive life and the ultimate purpose of life at one and the same time. And this uncertainty haunts the field of biology, rendering it also increasingly speculative, as each further discovery is made – not through some temporary incapacity on the part of science, but because it is approaching the definitive uncertainty which is its absolute horizon.

The transcription and 'objective' assessment of an overall system have, ultimately, no more meaning than the assessment of the weight of the earth in millions of billions of tons – a figure which has no meaning outside of a calculation internal to the terrestrial system.

Metaphysically, it is the same: the values, purposes and causes we delineate are valid only for a form of thought which is human, all too human. They are irrelevant to any other reality whatever (perhaps even to 'reality' *tout court*).

The sphere of the real is itself no longer exchangeable for the sphere of the sign. As with floating currencies, the relationship between the two is growing undecidable, and the rate at which they exchange increasingly random. Both are becoming speculative, each in its own space. Reality is growing increasingly technical and efficient; everything that can be done is being done, though without any longer meaning anything. And the metalanguages of reality (the human and social sciences, technical and operational languages) are also developing eccentrically, after the fashion of their objects. As for the sign, it is passing into the pure speculation and simulation of the virtual world, the world of the total screen, where the same uncertainty hovers over the real and 'virtual reality' once they go their separate ways. The real no longer has any force as sign, and signs no longer have any force of meaning.

Any system invents for itself a principle of equilibrium, exchange and value, causality and purpose, which plays on fixed oppositions: good and evil, true and false, sign and referent, subject and object. This is the whole space of difference and regulation by difference which, as long as it functions, ensures the stability and dialectical movement of the whole. Up to this point, all is well. It is when this bi-polar relationship breaks down, when the system short-circuits itself, that it generates its own critical mass, and veers off exponentially. When there is no longer any internal reference system within which exchange can take place (between production and social wealth, for example, or between news coverage and real events), you get into an exponential phase, a phase of speculative disorder.

The illusion of the economic sphere lies in its having aspired to ground a prin-ciple of reality and rationality on the forgetting of this ultimate reality of impossible exchange. Now, that principle is valid only within an artificially bounded sphere. Outside that sphere lies radical uncertainty. And it is this exiled, foreclosed uncer-tainty which haunts systems and generates the illusion of the economic, the political, and so on. It is the failure to understand this which leads systems into incoherence, hypertrophy and, in some sense, leads them to destroy themselves. For it is from the inside, by overreaching themselves, that systems make bonfires of their own postulates, and fall into ruins.

To put it another way: has there ever been any 'economy', in the sense of an organization of value that is stably coherent and has a universal purpose and mean-ing? In absolute terms, the answer is no. Has there ever even been a 'real'? In this chasm of uncertainty, the real, value and the law are exceptions, exceptional phe-nomena. Illusion is the fundamental rule.

Everything which sets out to exchange itself for something runs up, in the end, against the Impossible Exchange Barrier. The most concerted, most subtle attempts to make the world meaningful in value terms, to endow it with meaning, come to grief on this insuperable obstacle. And that which cannot be exchanged for any-thing else proliferates wildly. The most structured systems cannot but be thrown out of kilter by the reversion of this Nothing which haunts them. And not in the aftermath of some future catastrophe, but right now. Here and now, the whole edifice of value is exchangeable for Nothing.

The true formula of contemporary nihilism lies here, rather than in any philosophical or moral considerations: it is the nihilism of value itself. This is our fate, and from this stem both the happiest and most baleful consequences. This book might be said to be the exploration, first, of the 'fateful' consequences, and subsequently – by a poetic turnabout – of the fortunate, happy consequences, of impossible exchange.

Behind the exchange of value and, in a sense, serving as an invisible counterpart to it, behind this mad speculation which reaches a peak in the virtual economy, behind the exchange of Something, we have, then, always, the exchange of the Nothing.

Death, illusion, absence, the negative, evil, the accursed share are everywhere, running beneath the surface of all exchanges. It is even this continuity of the Nothing which grounds the possibility of the Great Game of Exchange. All current strategies boil down to this: passing around the debt, the credit, the unreal, unnameable thing you cannot get rid of. Nietzsche analysed the stratagem of God in these terms: in redeeming man's debt by the sacrifice of His son, God, the great Creditor, created a situation where the debt could never be redeemed by the debtor, since it has already been redeemed by the creditor. In this way, He created the possibility of an endless circulation of that debt, which man will bear as his perpetual sin. This is the ruse of God. But it is also the ruse of capital, which, at the same time as it plunges the world into ever greater debt, works simultaneously to redeem that debt, thus creating a situation in which it will never be able to be cancelled or exchanged for anything. And this is true also of the Real and the Virtual: the endless circulation of the Virtual will create a situation where the Real will never be able to be exchanged for anything.

If it is the forgetting and denial of the Nothing which brings about the catastrophic deregulation of systems, there is no way of warding off this process by the magical addition of some *ex machina* corrective – the kind of regulation we see at work in the physical, biological and economic sciences, where new hypotheses, new forces and new particles are constantly being invented to shore up the equations. If it is the Nothing whose absence is missing, it is the Nothing which must be brought (or returned) into play, with the attendant risk of internal catastrophe being constantly present.

The irruption of radical uncertainty into all fields and the end of the comforting universe of determinacy is not at all a negative fate, so long as uncertainty itself becomes the new rule of the game. So long as we do not seek to correct that uncertainty by injecting new values, new certainties, but have it circulate as the basic rule. It is the same here as with the will: you can resolve the problem of the will only by a (poetic) transference into the play of otherness, without ever claiming to resolve the question of its ends and its object. It is on the continuity and reciprocal exchange of the Nothing, of illusion, of absence, of non-value, that the continuity of Something is founded.

Uncertainty in this sense becomes the very precondition for the divided nature of thought. Just as uncertainty in physics arises in the end from the fact that the object, in its turn, analyses the subject, so the uncertainty of thought comes from the fact that I am not alone in thinking the world – that the world, in its turn, thinks me.

The Nothing is the only ground – or background – against which we can apprehend existence. It is existence's potential of absence and nullity, but also of energy (there is an analogy here with the quantum void). In this sense, things only ever exist *ex nihilo*. Things only ever exist out of nothing.

The Nothing does not cease to exist as soon as there is something. The Nothing continues (not) to exist just beneath the surface of things. This is Macedonio

Fernandez's 'perpetual continuation of the Nothing'. Everything which exists continues, then, not to exist at the same time. This antinomy is beyond the imagining of our critical understanding.

Ex nihilo in nihilum: this is the cycle of the Nothing. It is also – against a thinking based on origins and ends, on evolution and continuity – a discontinuity-based thinking. Only the consideration of an end allows us to conceive a continuity, and our sciences and technologies have accustomed us to see everything in terms of a continuous evolution, which is never anything other than our own – the theological form of our superiority. The essential form, however, is that of discontinuity.

Everywhere in the universe, discontinuity alone is probable. The Big Bang itself is the absolute model. Might it not be the same for living things, events, language? Infinitesimal as is the passage from one form to another, it is always a jump, a catastrophe – from which the strangest, most anomalous forms ensue unexpectedly, with no regard for the end result. Closer to home, languages also provide a fine example of this singular discontinuity (from one signifier to the other, one language to the other), developing in largely random manner, without any continuous progress or superiority of one over another.

For analytical thought, the evolution and advance of living forms is the only possible hypothesis. If the world has a history, then we can aspire to a final explanation of it. But, as Cioran says, 'if life has a meaning, we are all failures'. In other words, the finalistic hypothesis is a despairing one. It emphasizes our failure, and plunges us into an unhappy uncertainty. On the other hand, if the world emerged at a single stroke, it cannot have any determinate meaning or end. We are protected from its end by this non-meaning which assumes a force of poetic illusion. The world, admittedly, then becomes wholly enigmatic, but this uncertainty, like that of appearances, is a happy uncertainty. Illusion, being *par excellence* the art of appearing, of emerging out of nothing, protects us from *being*. As the art of disappearance, it protects us from death. The world is protected from its end by its diabolical indeterminacy.

According to this other hypothesis, the biomass emerged at a stroke. It has been here in its entirety from the beginning: the subsequent history of its complex forms changes nothing about the Big Bang of life. Things here are exactly as they are with the universe, where everything was present in the primal instant. Exactly as it is for language in Lévi-Strauss's thinking: the logomass, the mass of language, emerges in its entirety at a stroke. There will be no addition to it in terms of potential information. There is even too much information – an excess of signifier, which will (we hope) never be reduced. Once it has appeared, it is indestructible. As indestructible as the material substance of the world, or – closer to us – as the material substance of the sociological masses, whose equally sudden appearance is also irreversible (until their eventual collapse, which is as unpredictable, from our limited standpoint, as was their appearance).

Astromass, biomass, logomass, sociomass, semiomass – all are doubtless destined to end one day. Yet they will end not gradually, but suddenly, the way they appeared. Like cultures, which are also invented at a stroke. Their emergence is inexplicable in evolutionary terms, and they sometimes disappear for no visible reason, like living species.

As for our mental universe, it no doubt functions according to this same catastrophic rule: everything is there from the beginning; it is not negotiated by stages. It is like a set of rules: perfect in itself; any idea of progress or change is absurd. It emerges *ex nihilo*; it can disappear only *ex abrupto*. This suddenness, this emergence out of the void, this non-anteriority of things to themselves continue to affect the event of the world at the very heart of its historical unfolding. What constitutes an event is what breaks with all prior causality. The event of language is what makes it re-emerge miraculously every day, as finished form, outside of all prior significations, even outside its current meaning – as though it had never existed. Gosse's hypothesis and Russell's paradox.[1]

And, in the end, we prefer the *ex nihilo*. We prefer something which draws its magic from arbitrariness, from the absence of causes and history. Nothing gives us greater pleasure than something emerging or disappearing at a stroke, than plenitude giving way to the void. Illusion is made of this magic portion, this accursed share, which creates a kind of absolute gain by removing causes, or by distorting effects and causes.

The fundamental uncertainty lies in this machination of the Nothing, in this parallel machinery of the Nothing.

The illusion of having 'overcome' this uncertainty is a mere phantasm of the understanding – a phantasm which lurks behind all value systems and representations of an objective world, including the traditional philosophical question: 'Why is there Something rather than Nothing?' Whereas the true question should, rather, be: 'Why is there Nothing rather than Something?'

But, then, if Nothing is the underlying fabric of all things, it is safely there for eternity, and it profits us 'nothing' to concern ourselves overmuch either with it or

---

1. Here Baudrillard is referring not to what is commonly termed 'Russell's paradox' (a proposition in set theory), but to Russell's argument in *The Analysis of Mind*: 'There is no logical impossibility in the hypothesis that the world sprang into being five minutes ago, exactly as it then was, with a population that "remembered" a wholly unreal past.' The nineteenth-century English naturalist P.H. Gosse actually contended that all geological and fossil findings were merely a simulation contemporaneous with the creation of the world by God five thousand years ago – a contention clearly designed to rescue the biblical account.

with the apparent hegemony of an objective world. Come what may, the Nothing will recognize its own. But the Nothing is precisely not a state of things. It is the product of the dramatic illusion of appearances. And it is the predestined target of the truth enterprise, the enterprise of verifying and objectifying the world – a gigantic homeopathic treatment of the world with the single reality-principle – putting an end to that dramatic illusion, putting an end, with a definitive coherence, to the divine incoherence of the world, an incoherence which is not measured against its own end, and which, indeed, is measured against Nothing.

Not to mention the fact that if this 'dark matter' did not exist, our universe would long ago have vanished into thin air. And this is, indeed, the most likely outcome if we succeed in eliminating it. Wherever this void – this antagonistic parallel universe, this radical illusion irreducible to the facts of the real and the rational – is eliminated, the real meets with immediate catastrophe. For matter in itself is a delusion, and the material universe is supported only by the missing mass, whose absence is decisive. The real divested of the anti-real becomes hyperreal, more real than the real, and vanishes into simulation. Matter divested of anti-matter is doomed to entropy. By elimination of the void, it is condemned to gravitational collapse. The subject deprived of all otherness collapses into itself, and sinks into autism. The elimination of the inhuman causes the human to collapse into odium and ridicule (this we see in the pretension and vanity of humanitarianism).

There is a very fine parable for this situation in the story of Ishi. Ishi, the last Indian of his tribe, who was taken to San Francisco, was stupefied by the sight of the vast crowds there. He could think only that the dead – all the previous generations – were also there among the living. And the dead, indeed, shield us from being continually present one to another. If you eliminate the dead, then, by dint of sheer overcrowding, the living become strangers to one another. This is what happens in our state of urban overpopulation, overinformation, overcommunication:

the whole space is suffocated by this hyper-presence. This is the mass state, where only the living dead remain.

However, the question remains: why are we so intent on ferreting out and destroying the void, absence and death? Why this fantasy of expelling the dark matter, making everything visible, making it real, and forcibly expressing what has no desire to be expressed, forcibly exhuming the only things which ensure the continuity of the Nothing and of the secret? Why are we so lethally tempted into transparency, identity and existence at all costs? An unanswerable question. But perhaps this tendency to be done with all secrets has itself a secret purpose?

In the past, through Creation and Nature, God was quite naturally the instigator of Good, as a providential transcendence worked itself out. God being naturally good, and mankind, in its modern, Rousseauist version, being basically good too, we did not have to transform the world to make it positive, and Evil was only ever an accident.

It is only since God died that the destiny of the world has become our responsibility. Since it can now no longer be justified in another world, it has to be justified here and now. The equivalent of the Kingdom of God – that is to say, the immanence of an entirely positive world (not the transcendence of an ideal world) – has to be brought about by technical means. And to create such an equivalent is, from the theological viewpoint, a total heresy. It is a diabolic temptation to wish for the Reign of Good, since to do so is to prepare the way for absolute Evil. If Good has a monopoly of this world, then the other will be the monopoly of Evil. We shall not escape the reversal of values, and the world will become the field of the metastases of the death of God.

Another explanation for our fall from grace is that the world is given to us. Now, what is given we have to be able to give back. In the past we could give thanks for the gift, or respond to it by sacrifice. Now we have no one to give thanks to. And if we can no longer give anything in exchange for the world, it is unacceptable.

So we are going to have to liquidate the given world. To destroy it by substituting an artificial one, built from scratch, a world for which we do not have to account to anyone. Hence this gigantic technical undertaking for eliminating the natural world in all its forms. All that is natural will be rejected from top to bottom as a consequence of this symbolic rule of the counter-gift and impossible exchange.

But, by this same symbolic rule, we are going to have to pay the price for this artificial creation, and settle this new debt towards ourselves. How are we to be absolved of this technical world and this artificial omnipotence if not by destruction, which is the only possible decompensation for this new situation – the only future event which will leave us with nothing to answer for?

So, all our systems are converging in a desperate effort to escape radical uncertainty, to conjure away the inevitable, fateful fact of impossible exchange. Commercial exchange, exchange of meaning, sexual exchange – everything has to be exchangeable. With all things, we have to find their ultimate equivalence, have to find a meaning and an end for them. When we have that end, that formula, that purpose, then we shall be quits with the world; all will be 'redeemed', the debt will be paid, and radical uncertainty will come to an end. Up to now, all systems have failed. The magical, metaphysical, religious systems which worked in the past are now a dead letter. *But this time we seem to have the final solution, the definitive equivalent: Virtual Reality in all its forms* – the digital, information, universal computation, cloning. In short, the putting in place of a perfect virtual, technological artefact, so that the world can be exchanged for its artificial double. A much more radical solution than all the others, this, since it will no longer have to be exchanged for some transcendence or finality from elsewhere, but for itself, by the substitution of a double which is infinitely 'truer', infinitely more real than the real world – thus putting an end to the question of reality, and to any inclination to give it a meaning. An automatic writing of the world in the absence of the world. Total equivalence, total screen, final solution. Absolutely consolidating the idea of the network as niche, into which it is so easy to disappear. The Internet thinks me. The Virtual thinks me. My double is wandering through the networks, where I shall never meet him. For that parallel universe has no relation to this one. It is an artificial transcription of it, a total echoing of it, but it does not reflect it. The Virtual is no longer the potentially real, as once it was. Non-referential – orbital and exorbital – it is never again intended to meet up with the real world. Having absorbed the original, it produces the world as undecidable.

But is not this parallel universe, which is based on the disappearance of the other, itself doomed to disappear, and is it not itself prey to undecidability? Perhaps it is simply an outgrowth of this world, playfully duplicating itself, in which case this world continues to exist as it is, and we are merely play-acting the Virtual? In the same way as, with the religious 'ulterior worlds', we were play-acting transcendence, though this time we would be play-acting immanence, operational power, play-acting *la pensée unique* and the automatic writing of the world. In other words, here again, a system doomed to fail, a phantasmagoria without the power to ward off the uncertainty and deregulation which ensued from impossible exchange.

In our general anthropology, there is meaning only in what is Human. The story has meaning only when it fits into some unfolding of events, some rational purpose. There is no reason in history, no reason in Reason, except as part of this triumphant evolutionism.

Measuring life by its meaning.

Measuring the world by the Human.

Measuring the event by History.

Measuring thought by the Real.

Measuring the sign by the thing, and so on.

Instead of *measuring oneself* against the world, measuring oneself against the event, measuring oneself against thought. . . .

We are moving everywhere towards an elimination of the Inhuman, towards an anthropological integrism which aims to submit everything to the jurisdiction of the Human. This is an enterprise of hominization which has been extended to animals, nature, and all other species under the banner of human rights, a moral anthropology and a universal ecology – this latter spearheading a campaign to annex the Inhuman to the *pensée unique* of the Human. A planetary project to exterminate the Inhuman in all its forms, an integrist project to domesticate any reality from outside our own sphere – the extreme turn of an imperialism by which, ironically and paradoxically, we deprive ourselves of any idea of the Human as such. For this can come to us only from the Inhuman. It is only on the basis of a radical alteration of our viewpoint that we can have a vision of ourselves and the world – not to fall into a universe of non-meaning, but to recover the potency and originality of the world before it assumes force of meaning and becomes, in that same movement, the site of all powers.

Thought itself must play its part in this process. It must register a leap, a mutation, an intensification. The point is no longer to throw the system into internal contradiction (we know that it regenerates in this spiral of contradiction), but to destabilize it by the infiltration of a viral – or, in other words, inhuman – thought, a thought which lets itself be thought by the Inhuman.

Ultimately, is not thought already a form of the Inhuman, a luxurious dysfunction which contravenes the evolution of life in general by taking stock of that evolution and trapping it in its own image? Does not the neuronal development of the brain already constitute a critical threshold from the point of view of evolution and the species? Then why not speed up the process and precipitate other concatenations, other forms – forms of an objective fate of which we simply have no inkling?

This exclusion of the Inhuman means that from now on it is the Inhuman which thinks us. We can grasp the world only from an omega point external to the Human, from objects and hypotheses which play, for us, the role of strange attractors. Thought has already run up against these kinds of objects at the margins of the inhuman in the past – as, for example, when it came up against primitive societies. Today, however, we have to look further than this critical thinking, a derivative of Western humanism, to far stranger objects which are bearers of a radical uncertainty, and on which we can no longer impose our perspectives in any way whatever.

The convergence of thought is no longer a convergence with truth, but a collusion with the object and a convergence with a set of rules in which the subject is no longer in control.

And what of all these hypotheses themselves which are advanced here? Do they have an equivalent, a use-value, an exchange-value? Absolutely not; it is impossible to exchange them. They can only stike at the chinks in the world's defences, and thought cannot but destroy itself in the object which thinks it, at the same time as it destroys the object it thinks. This is how it escapes truth. Now we have, at the very least, to escape truth. And to escape truth, you must not, whatever you do, trust the subject. You have to leave matters to the object and its strange attraction, the world and its definitive uncertainty.

The whole problem is one of abandoning critical thought, which is the very essence of our theoretical culture, but which belongs to a past history, a past life.

The conventional universe of subject and object, ends and means, true and false, good and evil, no longer matches up to the state of our world. The 'normal' dimensions − of time, space, determination, representation, and hence also of critical, reflexive thought − are deceptive. The discursive universe of psychology, sociology and ideology in which we move is a trap. It is still functioning in a Euclidean dimension. Now, we have almost no theoretical intuition of what has, without realizing it, become a quantum universe − just as we have never had anything but a dim theoretical awareness of the order of simulation into which our modern world long ago unwittingly passed, while retaining a blind faith in the idea of an objective reality. I would even say that it is this superstitious belief in − this hysteresis of − the 'real' and the reality principle that is the true imposture of our times.

We analysed a deterministic society deterministically. Today we have to analyse a non-deterministic society non-deterministically − a fractal, random, exponential society, the society of the critical mass and extreme phenomena, a society entirely dominated by relations of uncertainty.

Everything in this society stands under the sign of uncertainty. As a consequence, we can no longer approach it in terms of social determinacy, even if we were to do so critically. Crisis always brought with it its share of tensions and contradictions; it is the natural movement of our history. But we are no longer in crisis; we are in a catastrophic process − not in the sense of a material apocalypse, but in the sense of an overturning of all rules. Catastrophe is the irruption of something which no longer functions according to the rules, or functions by rules we do not know, and perhaps never will. Nothing is simply contradictory or irrational in this state; everything is paradoxical. To pass beyond the end − into the excess of reality, the excess of positivity, the excess of events, the excess of information − is to enter a paradoxical state, a state which can no longer be content with a rehabilitation of traditional values, and demands a thinking that is itself paradoxical: a thinking that no longer obeys a truth principle, and even accepts the impossibility of verification.

We have passed beyond a point of no-return, and beyond this things develop along quite other lines. Ideas of linear development no longer apply. Everything is cast into a turbulence which makes control impossible, including the control of time, for the simultaneity of world information — that transparency of all places brought together in a single moment — is not unlike a perfect crime perpetrated on time.

The uncertainty principle, which states that it is impossible to calculate the speed of a particle and its position simultaneously, is not confined to physics. It applies also to the impossibility of evaluating both the reality and the meaning of an event as it appears in the information media, the impossibility of distinguishing causes and effects in a particular complex process — of distinguishing the terrorist from the hostage (in the Stockholm syndrome), the virus from the cell (in viral pathology). This is just as impossible as isolating subject from object in experiments in sub-atomic physics. Each of our actions is at the same erratic stage as the microscopic particle: you cannot evaluate both its end and its means. You can no longer calculate both the price of a human life and its statistical value. Uncertainty has seeped into all areas of life. And this is not a product of the complexity of parameters (we can always cope with that); it is a definitive uncertainty linked to the irreconcilable character of the data. If we cannot grasp both the genesis and the singularity of the event, the appearance of things and their meaning, then two courses are open to us: either we master meaning, and appearances escape us; or the meaning escapes, and appearances are saved. By the very play of appearances, things are becoming further and further removed from their meaning, and resisting the violence of interpretation.

However this may be, we live in the real and in the order of rational determination, but we do so as though these things represented a 'state of exception'. We live in a double bind: with a dual allegiance, a dual obligation. We live, for the most part, in a Newtonian universe, but we are governed basically by non-determinist equations. Is there no getting over this disparity? Things are the same in social physics as in the physics of nature: macroscopic phenomena still conform to a deterministic analysis, but microscopic phenomena do not behave in any such way. At the level of physical processes, no flagrant contradictions occur: we get along very well in a Newtonian universe. But in the social and historical world, the world of relationships, the mismatch between behaviour and analysis is becoming blatant. A whole area of social functioning still corresponds to a deterministic analysis, a 'realist' sociology (Marxist, empiricist, behaviourist or statistical), and we operate in large measure in this register of the 'real'. But, simultaneously, another kind of functioning – probabilistic, relativistic, aleatory – is gaining the upper hand, and the 'realist' area is secretly immersed in this. In this de-polarized social space (is it still a social or historical space?), traditional analysis no longer has any purchase, and solutions worked out at this level come to grief on a general uncertainty in the same way as classical calculations come to grief in quantum physics.

There is no longer any social determinism. The increase in speed renders all positions improbable. In a field of exclusion, you cannot calculate both the current position of an individual and his or her velocity of exclusion. With a particular type of work or status (or particular kinds of stocks and shares), you cannot calculate both the real value and the rate of devaluation. With entire categories, you cannot calculate both their advancement and their virtual downgrading (as if by chance, the advancement of women is accompanied by a creeping disqualification of the occupations concerned, which cancels out the social advantage gained). With signs, you cannot calculate both their sense and their obsolescence. And with anything in general, you cannot calculate both its effect in real time and its duration. So it is with the indeterminacy of the social.

Hitherto, priority has been given to the analysis of determinate historical forms, in terms of distinct oppositions, such as capital and labour. Today, however, the sphere of labour has become hazy, and the concept itself has lost its definition. As Canetti says of history, we have passed beyond the 'blind point' of the social, and also imperceptibly beyond capital and labour and their antagonistic dynamic. The social machine now moves in a general cycle or, rather, on a Moebius strip, and the social actors are always on both sides of the contract.

The term 'social fracture' is itself part of an attempt to rehabilitate the old objective conditions of capital and labour. Just as the nineteenth-century utopians tried, in a period of industrial boom, to revive values associated with the land and with craft work, so we are trying, in an age of information technology and virtual reality, to revive the social conflicts and relations associated with the industrial era. The same utopia, the same optical illusion. And if the golden age of relations of force and dialectical contradictions has to go, that is just too bad. Marx's analysis itself was of the order of a deterministic simplification of conflicts and history, but it was linked to an ascending curve, and to the possibility of a determinate negation: the social and the proletariat were still concepts destined to surpass and negate themselves. They bore no relation to the positivistic mystification of the social and of labour in our current context. What is lost in our 'interactivist' sociality is precisely the negative element, and the possibility of a determinate negation of the objective conditions. There are no 'objective conditions' any more. More generally, the virtuality of information no longer offers the possibility of a determinate negation of reality. There is no 'objective' reality any more. We may as well accept this, and stop dreaming of a situation that is long dead. We are no longer in the negative and in history, we are in a state where relations of force and social relations have more or less yielded their vitality to a virtual interface and a diffuse collective performance at the point where all speculative flows intersect – flows of employment, capital flows, information flows. But we have to regard this situation as an unprecedented one, and if history has become – as Marx put it – a farce, it might well be that that farce, by reproducing itself, may become our history.

A painful revision of the reality principle, a painful revision of the principle of knowledge. This latter assumes the existence of a dialectic between subject and object, with the subject in control, since he invents it.

Now, the rules of the game have only to change, or become uncertain, or we have only to lose control of the principles, or the object has only to refuse to allow itself to be decoded in the terms we have laid down, for knowledge to become metaphysically impossible. And this is not simply a *metaphysical* impossibility: right now, the sciences are incapable of according a definite status to their object.

The object is not what it was. In all areas it evades us. It now appears only as a fleeting trace on computer screens. At the end of their experimenting, the most advanced sciences can only register its disappearance. Are we not faced here with an ironic revenge of the object, a strategy of deterrence, flouting experimental protocols and divesting the subject itself of its subject position?

Ultimately, science has never stopped churning out a reassuring scenario in which the world is being progressively deciphered by the advances of reason. This was the hypothesis with which we 'discovered' the world, atoms, molecules, particles, viruses, and so forth. But no one has ever advanced the hypothesis that things may discover us at the same time as we discover them, and that there is a dual relationship in discovery. This is because we do not see the object in its originality. We see it as passive, as waiting to be discovered – a bit like America being discovered by the Spaniards. But things are not like that. When the subject discovers the object – whether that object is viruses or primitive societies – the converse, and never innocent, discovery is also made: the discovery of the subject by the object. Today, they say that science no longer 'discovers' its object, but 'invents' it. We should say, then, that the object, too, does more than just 'discover' us; it invents us purely and simply – it thinks us. It seems that we have victoriously wrenched the object from its peaceful state, from its indifference and the secrecy which enshrouded it. But today, before our very eyes, the enigmatic nature of the world is rousing itself, resolved to struggle to retain its mystery. Knowledge is a duel. And this duel between subject and object brings with it the subject's loss of sovereignty, making the object itself the horizon of its disappearance.

At any rate, it seems that reality, indifferent to any truth, cares not one jot for the knowledge to be derived from observing and analysing it. A docile – if not, indeed, hyper-docile – reality bends to all hypotheses, and verifies them all without distinction. For reality, it is all merely a superficial and provisional 'enframing' [*Gestell*] in the Heideggerian sense. Reality itself has become simulative, and leaves us with a sense of its fundamental unintelligibility, which has nothing mystical about it, but would seem, rather, to be ironic. Having reached the paroxystic state (which is, as the name implies, the state just before the end), reality slips over of its own accord into the parodic – irony and parody being the last glimmer reality sends out to us before disappearing, the last sign the object sends out to us from the depths of its mystery.

Critical thought sees itself as holding up a mirror to the world, but the world knows no mirror stage. Thought must, then, go beyond this critical stage and reach the ulterior stage of the object which thinks us, the world which thinks us. That object-thought is no longer reflective, but reversible. It is merely a special case in the succeeding states of the world, and no longer has the privilege of universality.

It has no privilege whatsoever in respect of the incomparable event of the world (though it doubtless has the charm of singularity). It is, in any event, irreducible to the consciousness of the subject. In the disorder of the world, thought, as an exceptional attribute and destiny of the species, is too precious to be reduced to the consciousness of the subject. There could be said, then, to be an interplay between thinking and the world which has nothing to do with the exchange of truth – and which, indeed, might even be said to suppose such exchange impossible.

Object-thought, thought become inhuman, is the form of thinking which actually comes to terms with impossible exchange. It no longer attempts to interpret the world, nor to exchange it for ideas; it has opted for uncertainty, which becomes its rule. It becomes the thinking of the world thinking us. In so doing, it changes the course of the world. For though there is no possible equivalence between thought and the world, there does occur, beyond any critical point of view, a reciprocal alteration between matter and thought. So the situation is reversed: if, once, the subject constituted an event in the world of the object, today the object constitutes an event in the universe of the subject. If the sudden emergence of consciousness constituted an event in the course of the world, today the world constitutes an event in the course of consciousness, in so far as it now forms part of its material destiny, part of the destiny of matter, and hence of its radical uncertainty.

Physical alteration of the world by consciousness, metaphysical alteration of consciousness by the world: there is no cause to ask where this begins, or 'who thinks whom'. Each is simultaneously in play, and each deflects the other from its goal. Has not humanity, with its inborn consciousness, its ambiguity, its symbolic order and its power of illusion, ended up altering the universe, affecting or infecting it with its own uncertainty? Has it not ended up contaminating the world (of which it is, nevertheless, an integral part) with its non-being, its way of not-being-in-the-world?

This raises many questions regarding the pertinence of knowledge – and not only classical knowledge but quantum, probabilistic science too, since, above and beyond the experimentation which alters its object – now cited as a commonplace example – man is faced in all registers with a universe altered and destabilized by thought. The hypothesis has even been advanced (Diran) that, if there were objective laws of the universe, it is because of humankind that they could neither be formulated nor operate in fact. Rather than humanity bringing reason into a chaotic universe, it would be the bringer of disorder, by its act of knowledge, of thought, which constitutes an extraordinary *coup de force*: establishing a point (even a simulated one) outside the universe from which to see and reflect (on) the universe. If the universe is what does not have a double, since nothing exists outside it, then the mere attempt to make such a point exist is tantamount to a desire to put an end to it.

The Final Solution
or
The Revenge of the Immortals

This final solution is, in fact, our deepest fantasy and the fantasy of our science. A fantasy of immortality by deep-freezing or cryogenics, or by replication and cloning in all its forms.

The most famous example is obviously Walt Disney in his coffin of liquid nitrogen. But at least he, with his whole body cryogenized, has the prospect of being resurrected whole. Other variants are appearing today which are so many experimental chimeras. In Phoenix, Arizona, for example – a place predestined for rebirth (from one's ashes) – only bodiless heads are now cryogenized, since the hope is to resuscitate individuals in their entirety from the brain, regarded as the core of the individual. By contrast with these cephaloid beings, in some laboratories across the Atlantic headless mice and frogs are being cloned, the intention being later to clone headless human beings which will serve to provide substitute organs. Since the head is regarded as the site of consciousness, it is better to manufacture headless creatures, so as to be able freely to use their organs without too many moral and psychological difficulties.

These are some of the forms of experimental cloning; but there is also cloning – and hence automatic immortality – in nature. It lies in the heart of our cells.

Normally, these cells are destined to divide a certain number of times, then die. If, during these divisions, a disturbance occurs (an impairment of the anti-tumour gene, or of the function of apoptosis), the cell becomes cancerous: *it forgets to die*, it forgets how to die. It will clone itself in billions of identical copies, forming a tumour. Usually, the subject dies and the cancerous cells die with him. But in the case of Henrietta Lacks,[1] tumour cells removed during her lifetime were grown on in the laboratory, and continued to proliferate endlessly. Because they were particularly virulent, remarkable specimens, these cells were sent to all parts of the world, and even into space on *Discoverer 17*. Thus the disseminated body of Henrietta Lacks, cloned at the molecular level, continues on its immortal rounds many years after her death.

Something in us is hidden: death. But something else lurks in each of our cells: the act of forgetting to die. Immortality hovers ominously over us. We speak always of the struggle of life against death, not of the opposite danger. But we have to fight against the impossibility of dying. At the least let-up on the part of living beings in their struggle for death – their struggle for division, sex and otherness – they become indivisible again, self-identical, and hence immortal.

Contrary to everything we ordinarily believe, nature first created immortal

---

1. Henrietta Lacks, an African-American resident of Turner Station, Baltimore County, USA, died of cervical cancer in 1951 at Johns Hopkins Hospital. It was found that cells from her tumour were able to reproduce themselves outside the body, a process which is still not properly understood. These so-called 'HeLa' cells have been used in medical experiments throughout the world, and it is often argued that the polio vaccine could not have been created without them.

beings, and it was only by winning the battle for death that we became the living beings that we are. Blindly, we dream of defeating death and achieving immortality, whereas that is our most tragic destiny, a destiny inscribed in the previous life of our cells. It is this we are coming back to today in cloning (Freud's version of the death drive is simply this nostalgia for the unsexed, non-individuated states we knew before becoming mortal and discontinuous – true death being not so much the physical disappearance of the individual being as a regression towards a minimal state of undifferentiated living matter).

The evolution of the biosphere leads from immortals to mortals. In moving from absolute continuity to the subdivision of the selfsame – unicellular organisms – we gradually come closer to birth and death. Then the egg is fertilized by a sperm, and germinal cells specialize out: the organism produced is no longer the one or the other of its progenitors, but a peculiar combination of the two. We have moved from pure and simple reproduction to procreation. For the first time, the first two will die; and, for the first time, the third is born: we are at the stage of mortal, sexed, differentiated beings. The earlier order of viruses, of immortal beings, continues, but henceforth that world of eternal beings is encompassed within the world of mortals. The victory in evolution lies with mortal, discontinuous beings – with us. But things are not set in stone, and reversion to the earlier state is always possible. Not only in the viral revolt of cells, but in the present colossal undertaking, on the part of living beings themselves, to reconstruct a homogeneous, continuous universe – a continuum which in this case is artificial, in which, through our technical media and machinery, through our immense system of communications and information, we are building a perfect clone, an identical double of our world, a virtual replica of the world which heralds an endless replication.

We are currently reproducing and copying the cancer cell's pathological immortality in the individual and the species.

This is the revenge of the immortal, undifferentiated beings over mortal, sexed beings. It is this we may term the final solution.

After the great revolution in evolution which the coming of sex and death represented, we have before us the great involution – the involution which, through cloning and any number of other techniques, aims to free us from sex and death. Whereas living matter has done its utmost for millions of years to wrest things out of sameness, to wrench itself out of this kind of primitive entropy and incest, we are currently, through the very progress of science, re-creating the conditions for entropy and incest, and working on the disinformation of the species by cancelling out differences.

Here the question of the destiny of science arises. Does not its very progress lie on a (perverse) curve of evolution which could be said to lead to a total involution? And might not this final solution, towards which we are unconsciously working, be the secret destination of nature, and simultaneously that of all our efforts? This casts an unexpected light on everything we still regard today as a positive development.

The sexual revolution – the one and only sexual revolution – is that of the coming of sexuality in the evolution of living beings. The revolution of a duality putting an end to perpetual undividedness, to the perpetuity of the Same and its subdivision to infinity. It is, therefore, also the revolution of death. The opposite movement – ours – is the involutive movement of the species back beyond the revolution of the sexual and death. A colossal revisionist movement in the evolution of living matter.

Seen in this perspective, 'sexual liberation' is perfectly ambivalent. For though it seems to run in the same direction as the sexual revolution, of which it might be said to be the crowning glory, it turns out to be completely opposite to that revolution in its effects. The first phase is that of the dissociation of sexual activity from procreation: contraception, the pill, and so on. The second phase, even more fraught with consequences, is the dissociation of reproduction from sex. Sex had liberated itself from reproduction; today, reproduction is liberating itself from sex. Asexual, biotechnical reproduction, running from artificial insemination to full-blown cloning. This, too, is a form of liberation, but it is the complete opposite of the other. We were sexually liberated; now, we are liberated from sex or, in other words, virtually rid of the sexual function. In clones – and soon in humans too – sexuality, following upon its total liberation, becomes a useless function. Thus sexual liberation, the self-styled crowning glory of the evolution of sexed beings, marks, in its final consequences, the end of the sexual revolution. There is the same ambiguity here as with science. The benefits we had foreseen are inextricably intertwined with the harmful effects, or the perverse side-effects.

And death? Being linked to sex, it must, in some respects, meet the same fate. There is indeed a liberation of death which is contemporary with sexual liberation. Similarly, we attempt to dissociate life from death – conserving only life, of course, and making death a useless function which we should be able to do without, just as we can do without sex in reproduction. Deprogramming death as fateful event, as symbolic event, and including it from now on only as virtual reality, as an option, as an alternative in the software of living beings. Like that virtual reality of sex – cybersex – which awaits us in the future: as a kind of attraction, so to speak. All these functions which have become useless – sex, thought, death – will not disappear purely and simply, but will be recycled as leisure activities. It will be possible to preserve the – now useless – human being itself as an ontological attraction – a new variant of what Hegel called 'the self-propelling life of the dead [*das sich in sich selbst bewegende Leben des Todes*]'. From having been a vital function, death will become a luxury, a diversion. In a future civilization from which death has been eliminated, future clones might, perhaps, afford themselves the luxury of death, and become mortals once again in simulated form (cyberdeath).

Nature itself offers us a kind of anticipation of cloning in the form of twins and twinness: a mind-boggling situation of the reduplication of the same, of primitive symmetry, which we escape only by a breaking of − a break in − symmetry. But perhaps we have never entirely escaped this. And, with cloning, this hallucination of the twin from which we have never fully managed to separate ourselves might be said to re-emerge, at the same time as the fascination for a sort of archaic incest with this original double (for the dramatic consequences which ensue, see Cronenberg's film *Dead Ringers*).

Most of the time this twinness remains symbolic, but when it assumes material form it illustrates the mystery of that undivided separation that lies deep within us all (some have even claimed to find a biological trace of it). Hence, no doubt, the sacred, accursed character of twinness in all cultures and, as its converse, the eternal remorse of individuation. It is, in fact, with this 'ontological' break from the twin that individual being begins, and hence the possibility of otherness and a dual relation. Individuated beings we are − and proud of it − but somewhere, in an unconscious deeper than the psychological, we have never quite come to terms with this. . . . Do we not still hanker after this double, and − going even further back − do we not feel a yearning for all the many fellow beings from which we were wrenched during evolution? Is there not, where all this is concerned, an eternal remorse of individuation?

A double repentance, in fact: not just the repentance of individual emancipation from the species but, more deeply, sexed living beings repenting of leaving the inorganic realm. This is how it is. Any liberation whatsoever is experienced as anomie and betrayal, and hence as a source of interminable neurosis, more and more serious as we move away from that origin. It is difficult to bear freedom − difficult, perhaps, to bear life itself as a break with the inorganic chain of matter. This is the revenge of matter, of the species, of the immortal beings we thought we had won out over.

Should we not see this collective phantasm of a return to an undivided existence, to the destiny of undifferentiated living matter, this drift towards an in-different immortality, as the very form of the repentance of living matter in respect of the non-living? As an age-old repentance for a state that is past and gone, but has become, by virtue of – by the power of – our technologies, a form of silent compulsion?

Have we here a desire to put an end to the genetic randomness of differences, to put an end to the vagaries of living matter? Are we not tired of sex and difference, of emancipation and culture? The social and individual world offers many examples of this faltering, this resistance, or this nostalgic faithfulness to some earlier state. We are dealing with a kind of revisionism, a painful revision of the whole evolution of living matter and of the human species in particular – incapable of confronting its diversity, its complexity, its radical difference, its otherness.

But this may also be an adventure: pushing the artificialization of life as far as possible, to see what will survive this life-size experiment. If it turns out that not everything can be cloned, programmed, genetically and neurologically controlled, then what survives can truly be termed 'human' – an indestructible, inalienable form of the human. Naturally, in veering off down this experimental side-road, there is the danger that nothing will remain – the danger that the human will, purely and simply, be wiped out.

This was the experience of Biosphere II, the artificial synthesis of all the planet's data, the ideal duplication of the human species and its environment. In miniature, Biosphere II revealed the fact that the species and the entire planet (Biosphere I) had become their own virtual reality, that they had already been yielded up, beneath the giant geodesic dome of information, to a one-way experimental destiny. But can we still speak here of the human species? Is a species which aims to become artificially immortal, and to transform itself into pure information, still human?

Humankind has no prejudices: it is as happy to use itself as a guinea-pig as anything else, animate or inanimate. It will as happily gamble with the destiny of its own species as with that of all the others. In its blind will for greater knowledge, humanity is programming its own destruction with the same offhandedness, the same ferocity, as it is programming that of other species. It cannot be accused of greater egoism. Humanity is sacrificing itself to an experimental destiny unknown to the other species, which have hitherto been left to meet their natural fates. And whereas something like a self-preservation instinct seemed to be associated with that natural fate, this recent experimental destiny sweeps any such notion aside. A sign that, behind the ecological obsession with protection and conservation, which has more to do with nostalgia and remorse, a quite different trend has already won out: the trend towards the sacrifice of the species and unlimited experimentation.

A double, contradictory movement: alone of all species, the human being seeks to construct his immortal double – crowning natural selection with an artificial selection, which confers upon him an absolute privilege. But by that very act he puts an end to natural selection, which implied the death of each species, including his own, in accordance with the law of evolution. In this way he is breaking the symbolic rule and, in his haughty attempt to put an end to evolution, ushering in the involution of his own species, which is currently losing its own specificity, its natural immunity. The mortality of artificial species is even more rapid than that of natural species; hence, along these artificial paths, the human race is perhaps rushing even faster towards its end.

There is a very strange truth underlying all this: namely, that the human species seems to have trouble being reconciled with itself. In parallel with the violence it wreaks on others, it wreaks a violence of its own on itself – a violence in which it treats itself, here and now, as the survivor of a future catastrophe. As though, while being convinced of its own superiority, it were repenting of an evolution which has brought it to such a position of privilege and taken it, in a sense, beyond its end as a species. This moment is like the one Canetti identifies as the point when we passed out of history, except that here we are passing out of the species – and hence out of something even more fundamental. We are crossing a point beyond which nothing is human or inhuman any more (in Canetti's piece, this was the point beyond which nothing was true or false any more), and what is at stake here is no longer merely history lurching over into post-history, but the species lurching into the void.

Might not the human race, by some unexpected twist, rediscover that law of animal species which, at the critical point of saturation, automatically turn towards a form of collective suicide?

The inhumanity of the undertaking can be seen in the abolition of everything within us that is human, all too human: our desires, our deficiencies, our neuroses, our dreams, our disabilities, our viruses, our lunacies, our unconscious and even our sexuality – all the features which make us specific living beings – are now being ruled out of court. All genetic manipulation is haunted by an ideal model from which all negative traits are eliminated. So, in Biosphere II, an experimental prototype, there are no viruses, no germs, no scorpions, no sexual reproduction. Everything is expurgated, immunized, immortalized by transparency, disembodiment, disinfection, prophylaxis.

The reduction of life to survival is achieved by gradual reduction to the lowest common denominator – to the genome and the genetic inheritance – where it is the perpetual movement of the code which carries the day, and the distinctive signs of the human are effaced before the metonymic eternity of cells. The worst thing is that the living beings generated by their own formulae will undoubtedly not survive the process. What lives by the formula will die by the formula.

The boundaries between the human and the inhuman are indeed being wiped out. But we are transcending those boundaries not towards the superhuman and the transvaluation of values, but towards the subhuman and a disappearance of the very characteristics symbolic of the species. In the end, Nietzsche is being proved right: the human species, left to itself, can only duplicate or destroy itself.

The original humanism, the humanism of the Enlightenment, was based on the qualities of human beings, their natural gifts and virtues, their human essence, together with the right to have freedom and to exercise that freedom. Current humanism, in its extended version, is more concerned with conserving the organic being and the species. The justification for human rights no longer lies in a sovereign, moral being, but in the prerogatives of an endangered species. And with this shift these rights themselves become problematic, since the question arises of the rights of other species, other breeds, and of nature, against which those rights have to be defined. Now, is there a definition of the Human in genetic terms? And if such a thing existed, could a species have rights over its own genome, and over its potential genetic transformation? We share 98 per cent of our genes with the apes, and 90 per cent with mice. What rights does this shared heritage confer on apes and mice? Moreover, it seems that 90 per cent of the genes in our genome have no function. What right have those genes to exist? This is a crucial question, for if we decree that they are useless, we grant ourselves the right to eradicate them. And there is the same problem for any part of humanity itself: as soon as the human is no longer defined in terms of freedom and transcendence, but in terms of a biological equilibrium and functions, the specificity of human beings is eradicated and, with it, the specificity of humanism. Western humanism has already seen itself threatened once: by other cultures bursting on to the scene in the sixteenth century. At present, things are not giving way at the cultural level, but at that of the species: anthropological deregulation and simultaneous deregulation of all the moral, legal and symbolic rules that were those of humanism. Can we still speak of a soul and a conscience, can we speak of an unconscious, in view of the automata, clones and chimeras which will carry on the human species? Not just individual capital, but phylogenetic capital is threatened by this evaporation of the boundaries of the human – an evaporation not even into the inhuman, but into something which falls short of the human and the inhuman: the genetic simulation of life.

The respective interplay of the human and the inhuman has been halted, the balance between them destroyed. And, though the potential disappearance of the human is indeed a serious matter, the disappearance of the inhuman is every bit as grave. The specificity of everything that is not a human being, and of everything in human beings which is inhuman, is threatened by an emerging hegemony of the human in its highly modern, highly rational definition. Everywhere we see the desire to annex nature, animals, other races and cultures, to a universal jurisdiction. Everything is assigned its place in a hegemonic evolutionary anthropology, marking the positive triumph of a single-track conception of the human (in its Western definition, of course) in the name of the universal, the good, and democracy. Human rights are the engine of this anthropic, anthropocratic thinking today, behind which both the human and the inhuman proliferate in strict formal contradiction. And the result is a simultaneous re-emergence of human rights and human rights violations.

The other cultures do not make this distinction between the human and the inhuman. We invented it, and we are currently abolishing it – not in a higher synthesis, but by reduction to an undifferentiated technical abstraction, in accordance with the same dizzying prospect of a final solution.

★

We are told that whatever the genetic destiny of the clone, it will never be exactly the same as the original (naturally enough, since there will have been an original before it). Allegedly, we have nothing to fear from biological cloning, since culture already differentiates us in any case. Salvation is to be found in acquired characteristics, and in culture. They alone save us from infernal sameness. Now, it is, in fact, precisely the other way round. It is culture which clones us, and mental cloning precedes biological cloning by a long way. It is the acquired characteristic which clones us today culturally, under the banner of *la pensée unique*. It is through ideas, ways of life, the cultural context and milieu that our innate differences are most surely cancelled out. It is through the school system, the media system, the mass culture and information systems, that human beings become copies of each other. And it is this *de facto* cloning – social cloning, the industrial cloning of persons and things – which engenders the biological idea of the genome and genetic cloning, which is a mere ratification of mental and behavioural cloning.

This changes all thinking on prescriptive limits and the rights of the individual where scientific and technical experimentation is concerned. All the issues currently before the ethical committees and the collective consciousness, and all the speculation on them, have no meaning (other than a pseudo-moral and pseudo-philosophical meaning) when it is our culture of difference itself which acts most effectively to produce indifferentiation, the 'Human Xerox' and *la pensée unique*.

On the other hand, this whole business of cloning may have an unexpected side to it. For example, the clone may be seen as the parody of the original, its ironic, grotesque version. In that case, we may imagine all kinds of situations which might overturn our 'Oedipal' psychology. Such as the future clone killing his father, not in order to sleep with his mother – something which is impossible now, since there is only one parent-cell, and the father may very well be a woman – but to recover his status as an original. Or, conversely, the original, disqualified by his double, avenging himself on his clone. All kinds of conflicts which will be not between children and parents, but between the original and its double. We may even envisage an entirely new function of clones (one that runs counter to all the functions assigned to them today, which generally have to do with perpetuating life): they may be used to satisfy the death drive, the instinct of self-destruction. One will be able, for example, to kill off one's own clone and so destroy oneself without any really mortal risk: to commit suicide by proxy. But our biologists and moralists have not got round to this yet. They have not got to the point of seeing the death drive as a fact just as basic as immortality, though both are simultaneously in play in cloning – which by no means simplifies matters.

It has been one of the benefits of this enterprise more generally to reveal to us what any halfway-radical philosophy already knew: that there is no morality to set against this immoral desire, this technical desire for immortality. There are no laws of nature, nor is there any moral law which might be said to emanate from such laws. That is all an idealist vision which has, indeed, been perpetuated within science itself. There are, then, no natural rights or prohibitions which could base themselves on a division between Good and Evil. What is at stake here is not moral, but symbolic. There is a set of rules for living things; its form is secret and its purpose unexplained. Life is not 'worth' anything, not even human life. And if it is precious, it is precious not as a value, but as a form – an excessive and immoral form. Unexchangeable for any other life or value whatsoever. The human race itself is not exchangeable for any other artificial race of beings, even if that race were superior to it in value and performance.

Against the alleged immorality of cloning we should not, then, set an 'ethics of difference' and a humanistic, value-based morality. Cloning should be opposed, rather, with a superior immorality of forms. Not an abstract conception of law, but a vital exigency – which is the exigency of thought also, for thought, too, is a form which is not exchangeable for any objective purposive goal, or for its own artificial double. And this is how it can protect us.

So immortal creatures first ruled the earth, followed by the reign of mortal, sexed beings, which got the upper hand. But now the immortals are taking their silent revenge with all the techniques of cloning, artificial immortality and the marginalization of sex and death.

However, the outcome of the contest is not yet decided, and we can be sure of some fierce resistance from the mortals that we are – a resistance from the very depths of the species, consisting in a rejection of final solutions in all their forms.

Useless Functions

When the world, or reality, finds its artificial equivalent in the virtual, it becomes useless. When the only thing needed to reproduce the species is cloning, sex becomes a useless function. When everything can be encoded digitally, language becomes a useless function. When everything can be reduced to the brain and the neuronal network, the body becomes a useless function. When computer technology and the automatism of machines are all that is needed for production, work becomes a useless function. When, in the 'memory of water', the transference of the electromagnetic wave produces the same effects as the molecule itself, the molecule becomes useless. When time, and all its dimensions, are absorbed by real time, it becomes a useless function. When artificial memories reign supreme, our organic memories become superfluous (they are, in fact, gradually disappearing). When everything takes place between interactive terminals on the communication screen, the Other has become a useless function.

Now, how do things stand with the Other when it has disappeared? What does the Real become, what does the body become, when they have been supplanted by their operational formulae? What do sex, work, time and all the figures of otherness become when they fall prey to technological synthesis? What becomes of the event and history when they are programmed, broadcast and diluted to infinity in the media? Where the medium becomes highly defined, the substance becomes highly diluted.

It is the same with the living being when it is reduced to its 'abstract' (its DNA and its genetic code); what is to be done with this residual human being? What is to be done with the worker, once computerized work has been synthesized? This is not a new question: in Marx's writings, the question was what to do with human beings once their labour-power had been extracted. It has simply been radicalized to the point where it now embraces the whole of reality, which is slipping over into the area of that kind of waste we don't know how to dispose of.

Yet all these non-degradable things continue to exist, like the phantom extremities of an amputated limb. They are still running on inertia, like Jarry's Siberian ten-man bicycle, with its corpses which merely pedal ever faster — like Ballard's astronauts, long since dead, but circling the globe in perpetuity. Like those political and cultural institutions which carry on along their path into the void like headless chickens, or the high-wire artist who keeps on advancing down a wire that does not exist. Like the light of dead stars. Like the judgement of God, which is still there, even though God, too, died long ago.

The challenge to reality comes no longer from philosophical thought but from Virtual Reality and its techniques. Whereas thought put an end to the real in thought, the new technologies put an end to it in reality. Whereas thought works towards the un-completion of reality, the Virtual works towards the completion of the real and its final solution. The denial of reality which, in the philosophical dimension, was a mental operation becomes, with the technologies of the Virtual, a surgical one.

Of the Cheshire Cat there remains only the Smile.
Of the dream there remains only a memory trace.
Of the molecule there remains only the electromagnetic trace.
Of the real there remains only virtual reality.
Of the other there remains only a spectral form.

The 'memory of water' saga (Benveniste) is exemplary: the absent molecules producing effects, the electromagnetic waves dissociated from their substance, no molecular message remaining. Only the medium is efficient. This is the last stage of the transfiguration of the world into pure information, and hence of the general movement of our universe: high dilution of reality, the disappearance of any real source, which has now become useless.

From the virtual perspective, the real is only a vestige. It is merely a reference corpse. But so too are sex, work and the body: they are merely references now for the work of mourning, or for a diffuse melancholy. Something like s*audade*,[1] in the sense of a sorrow not for what is dead, but for what has disappeared. Now, the Real did not die a natural death; it simply disappeared, and we have only the vestiges of it. Or we know only how to tell its story – as in that fable in which the ancestors, in times of trouble or danger, knew where to go in the forest, how to make fire, how to perform the rite, but in the course of time the rite was lost, then the fire, then even the place, so that the descendants now know only how to tell the story. Today we tell ourselves the story of the Real, as once we told ourselves the stories of myth and the primal crime.

1. A mood of melancholic yearning, widely regarded as typically Portuguese. Connected with the myth of the lost king Sebastian, whose return is still awaited.

The Real – now unexchangeable because it has been spirited away by its double, but not ideologically degradable – becomes subject to endless demand, becomes an ideological concession granted in perpetuity. Work, disqualified as a productive function, is subjected to endless demand in the name of a 'right to work', an inalienable right to alienation itself (whereas, as the negative destiny of the industrial wage-slave, it was supposed to disappear).

Thus art, work, religion and the body, though dead, have forgotten to die. Since the gene presiding over their demise is masked for one reason or another, they are entering a 'phase beyond', an interminable phase. Wherever the process of apoptosis is blocked, we are in a world of entities which are virtually deceased, but have not yet found the agent of their demise.

Time itself – what are we to do with what remains to us, which now appears to us only in the form of ennui, that non-degradable residue? What are we to do with truth – the 'objective' world no longer has any time for truth – and all kinds of values of that sort? What are we to do with freedom, whose heart still beats weakly in a corner, like the digital clock on the Pompidou Centre? Who now cares a fig for it, since its dispersal into 'happiness' and the unconditional liberation of everything? Only the Idea of freedom still exists. Man and his freedom: phantom essences, holograms, for which Reality will be the theme park.

The destiny of all these things is to survive artificially, to be resurrected as reservation fetishes, like the animal species which are being 'rehabilitated', like the museified ghettos and all the things which survive in intensive care or on a drip-feed. There will always be horses, aborigines, children, sex, reality, but as an alibi, a fetish, a symbolic reservation, a décor, a privilege, a relic, a rare object – if not, indeed, an object of perversion (children). Protected species for well-calculated purposes of predation, to be enjoyed by some *in vivo* and consumed by others *in vitro*.

However, the dead – even the virtual dead – take their revenge. Time abolished in real time takes its revenge in the form of a frenzied millenarianism or the desperate search for origins. Nature reduced to an energy source takes its revenge in the form of natural catastrophes. The body conjured away into the virtual takes its revenge in the form of virality and autoimmune pathology. Foreclosed otherness returns in hatred, racism and lethal experimentation. The Real effaced by its double is a potentially dangerous ghost.

When you travel from Punta Arenas to Rio Grande in the south of Patagonia, for a hundred kilometres you skirt La Bahia Inútil – Useless Bay – where the sky is low, purple and immense, and the sheep have an air of night-owls about them. It is all so vast and so empty, so definitively empty, that it does not even merit a name; as though God had by some oversight cast this superfluous landscape down here – a landscape all the stranger for being part of an entire landmass, Patagonia, where all is useless and senseless.

Why, in this total solitude, create this additional bay, where there are no signs to decipher and nothing to detain the traveller? But to give it this name was also the most extraordinary homage one could have paid to a landscape, and the person who did so truly sensed the monotony of the hereafter – the supernatural end of all signification, the limbo world to which culture chose not to allot a proper name. Patagonia is rich in dramatic names – in Isles of Desolation, and so on – but all these seem very commonplace beside the term 'useless'. It occurs to you that truth itself would have deserved such a sublime epithet: 'Useless Truth'. And perhaps truth is in fact there – in those grey waters with that perpetual wind blowing over them.

The Impossible Exchange of One's Own Life

Our individual lives stand under the moral sign of a self-appropriation, and hence of a denial of all radical otherness, though that otherness makes its return in the form of the thwarted individual destinies that are our many neuroses and psychical disorders. In an age when all effects of will, freedom and responsibility pose an insoluble set of problems for us, and the liberation of energies, mores, sexes and desires is producing some noteworthy counter-effects; at a point when our entire culture, on the verge of the year 2000, is embarking on a painful revision in the face of the possibility of a final solution originating in science or history; at this moment of violent contradiction of the modern process of liberation, we have undoubtedly to go back to the origins to see whether this drive for liberation does not run counter to something even stronger, wilder, more primitive.

A battle would seem to be raging within us between the aspiration of an entire culture towards individual freedom and a repugnance for individuality and freedom stemming from somewhere deep in the species. And this contradictory movement finds expression in irresistible remorse, in deep resentment towards the world as it is, and in ever more intense self-hatred. The demand of the conscious mind is for greater and greater autonomy, for ever more freedom – by which we cut free from the conformism of traditional societies and, even more, from the archaic *enchaînement* of the species; by which we break the symbolic pact and the cycle of metamorphoses. Two kinds of violence ensue: a violence of liberation, and an opposite violence in reaction against the excess of freedom, safety, protection and integration, and hence against the loss of any dimension of fate, of destiny – a violence directed against the emergence of the Ego, the Self, the Subject or the Individual, which takes its toll in the form of self-hatred and repentance.

> This hatred of the present has not been well understood. Perhaps the first demand of emerging consciousness in this mass civilization is expressive. The spirit, released from servile dumbness, spits dung and howls with anguish stored during long ages. . . . In man, self-awareness has been accompanied at this stage with a sense of the loss of more general natural powers, of a price paid by instinct, by sacrifices of freedom, impulse (alienating labor, et cetera). The drama of this stage of human development seems to be the drama of disease, of self-revenge. An age of special comedy. What we see is not simply the leveling de Tocqueville predicted, but the plebeian stage of evolutionary self-awareness. Perhaps the revenge taken by numbers, by the species, on our impulses of narcissism (but also on the demand for freedom) is inevitable. In this new reign of multitudes, self-awareness tends to reveal us to ourselves as monsters. (Saul Bellow, *Herzog*)

The modern individual has crossed a critical threshold beyond which an original 'backlash' occurs on the part of the species – denial of self becoming the last stage of individual consciousness, just as, according to Nietzsche, *Ressentiment* is the last stage of the genealogy of morals. This is where the paradox and the perverse effects of all liberation – of what we call the advance of reason and civilization – crystallize. For this to happen, there is no need for a death drive, a biological nostalgia for a state prior to individuation and sex: it is our modern, paradoxical condition which produces this denial of self, this mortiferous repulsion. And indeed, death drive or no death drive (that immortality of protozoa), we are not far from rediscovering its equivalent today in the dimension of the clone as degree Xerox of the individual and degree Zero of evolution.

The question raised is, then, the question of destiny, of impossible destiny, of our collusion in the paradoxical destiny of a species haunted by the imagining of its own end. And the problem is no longer how to conquer freedom – how *are* we to conquer it? – but how to escape it. How are we to escape unchecked individuation and self-hatred? It is not how to escape our destiny, but how not to escape it? For we have lost the original. The destiny of the individual soul has lost much of its grandeur. In the past, the human being was not doomed to be merely what he is. God and Satan wrestled over him. In the past, we were important enough to have a battle fought over our souls. Today, our salvation is our own affair. Our lives are no longer marked by original sin but by the risk of failing to fulfil their ultimate potential: so we accumulate plans, ideals and programmes; we constantly pass the buck and seek to outdo each other in a universal effort to perform. And we subside into the condition of those who, as Kierkegaard put it, are no longer capable of facing the Last Judgement in person.

Since no one fights over our souls any longer, it is up to us to fight over ourselves, to put our own existences on the line, to be endlessly trying things out and competing in a perpetual, infernal contesting of ourselves – though there is no Last Judgement any more, and there are no longer any real rules.

In the final stage of his 'liberation' and emancipation through the networks, screens and new technologies, the modern individual becomes a fractal subject, both subdivisible to infinity and indivisible, closed on himself and doomed to endless identity. In a sense, the perfect subject, the subject without other – whose individuation is therefore not at all contradictory with mass status. Quite the contrary, indeed: he is the dispersal of the mass-effect into each individual parcel – each encapsulating in itself the seriality, the crazed [*étoilé*], metonymic structure of the mass, the characteristic feature of which is that it is at any one point substitutable for itself. Or, alternatively, the individual himself forms a mass – the mass structure being present, as in a hologram, in each individual fragment. In the virtual and media world, the mass and the individual are merely electronic extensions of each other. We have thus become virtual monads, free electrons, individuals left to ourselves, desperately seeking the other. But the particle has no other. The other particle is always the same. All that can exist is an anti-particle, which, on impact, would make the first particle disappear. Perhaps this is the only last eventuality there is: the destiny of the disappearance of matter into anti-matter, of sex into the other sex, of the individual into the mass. Reduced to nuclear identity, we no longer have any alternative destiny except a collision with our antagonistic double. This is, pretty much, the curse which afflicts the species – this latter breaking up first into individuals, then these in their turn breaking up into scattered particles by a process of inexorable fragmentation. Like matter, which saw itself split first into atoms, then into increasingly elusive particles – in such a way that you sense there will never be a final, truly elementary stage of matter, any more than there will be a definitive reference stage of the human being.

The modern individual, being no longer part of an order greater than himself, but a victim of his own will – commanded to be what he wants and to want what he is – ends up resenting himself, and, as a consequence, frittering himself away in the exhaustion of his possibilities: a new form of voluntary servitude. It is easy to understand why he may well ask nothing better than to lose that will and freedom, to hand over life-and-death discussions to anything else whatsoever. Any form at variance with individual being will enable him to escape the responsibility. Most often, however, the chosen forms of modification of the will and deviation of desire are mere parodies of fate. A fatal strategy this, then, but a derisory one. In the absence of transcendent powers watching over us, and in the perpetual effort to produce proof of our existence, we are forced to become '*fatal*' to ourselves. 'Deprived of destiny, the modern individual replaces it by a fateful experimentation on himself' (Sloterdijk).

This is how it is with all those who deliberately submit themselves to extreme conditions: solitary climbers or sailors, cavers and those who play jungle wargames. All risk-situations, which were once man's natural lot, are today re-created artificially in a form of nostalgia for extremes, survival and death. A technical simulation of pain and sacrifice – and this includes the humanitarian compulsion to take others' suffering on oneself in order to find in it a substitute destiny. Everywhere we find the same symbolic mortification. Stephen Hawking, brain of genius in a fallen body: the ideal mannequin of superscience. The plastic surgery undergone by Orlan[1] and so many others who experiment on and alter their bodies to the point of mutilation and torture. Handicaps, mutilations, prostheses, sexual fascination with accidents and lethal technologies (Cronenberg's *Crash*). Right down to 'boosting', that very specific method employed by the disabled athletes in the Atlanta Olympics who deliberately inflicted injury on themselves to improve their results. Not to mention drugs and other forms of mind-bending – anything goes in the

1. The French performance artist Orlan is noted for using plastic surgery on her own body as the vehicle of her art.

attempt to achieve this violent deconstruction of the body and thought. But experimentation occurs not only in the extreme cases. Behind every television and computer screen, every technical operation which confronts him daily, the individual is analysed in return, function by function. He is tested, experimented on, fragmented, harassed, summoned to respond: a fractal subject doomed henceforth to be disseminated in the networks. And the price to be paid is a mortification of the gaze, the body, and the real world.

With the media, polls, and all the checks and verifications which go on, we are living on a kind of perpetual test-bed (McLuhan), where the feedback is more or less automatic. We talk of sexual harassment, but it is all the social, psychological, political and mental promptings which are so many veiled forms of harassment, persecution and behavioural servitude. Through these, the individual reinvents for himself a form of *trompe-l'œil* destiny as the technical hallucination unfolds – a form of artificial danger through which each person defies himself to exist. Like those ascetics and anchorites of old who subjected themselves to all kinds of ordeals in the hope that God would respond to their bodily torments.

Thus, released from any fateful decree, deprived of any material adversity, modern individuals spend their lives putting their bodies and minds through a perpetual settling of accounts, daily inflicting the ordeal of the Last Judgement on themselves.

Beyond this derisory, compulsive identity – which is only ever the expiation, on the altar of technology and the sciences, of the refusal or loss of any symbolic belonging – is there not another form of destiny not to be escaped from? The path of a radical strangeness which breaks the vicious circle of identity; the path of a radical illusion which breaks the vicious circle of reality – destiny being, in the end, not that which opposes one's own will, but an impersonal will which enfolds one's own in its more subtle command.

An End to Freedom

Two spectres haunt the subject: the spectre of the Will and the spectre of Freedom. The pressure everywhere is for the subject to claim the full use of the one and the boundless exercise of the other. Today it is illegal to give up one's own will, or not to wish to be free.

The 'liberated' man becomes fully responsible for the objective conditions of his existence. This is, to say the least, an ambiguous destiny. In this way, the 'liberated' worker, for example, falls prey to the objective conditions of the labour market.

At the same time as it forms part of a movement of liberation (of energy, sex, mores and work), modernity also involves the transference of everything which had to do with the imagination, dreams, the ideal and utopia into a technical, operational reality: the materialization of all desires, the realization of all possibilities. Everything is accomplished unconditionally; there is no transcendence any more, no alienation. Fulfilled individuals, but fulfilled only virtually, of course. It is the virtual which renders reality total by absorbing any imaginary alternative. The individual at last becomes identical with himself; the promise of the ego has been fulfilled. The prophecy which was that of the whole of modern history, from Hegel and Marx to Stirner and the Situationists – the prophecy of the appropriation of self and the end of alienation – has been fulfilled. Not for better, but for worse. We have passed from the Other to the Same, from alienation to identification (similarly, the Nietzschean prophecy of the transvaluation of values has been fulfilled for the worse – not in our passing beyond Good and Evil, but in our falling back this side of Good and Evil).

This indivisible individual is the achieved utopia of the subject: the perfect subject, the subject without other. Without inner alterity, he is doomed to an endless identity. Self-identity of the individual, the subject, the nation, the race. Self-identity of the world, now technically and absolutely real – now 'become what it is'. No more metaphors, no more metamorphoses. All that remains is the indefinite metastasis of identity.

Identity is a dream that is pathetically absurd. You dream of being yourself when you have nothing better to do. You dream of yourself and gaining recognition when you have lost all singularity. Today we no longer fight for sovereignty or for glory, but for identity. Sovereignty was a mastery; identity is merely a reference. Sovereignty was adventurous; identity is linked to security (and also to the systems of verification which identify you). Identity is this obsession with appropriation of the liberated being, but a being liberated in sterile conditions, no longer knowing what he is. It is a label of existence without qualities. Now, all energies – the energies of minorities and entire peoples, the energies of individuals – are concentrated today on that derisory affirmation, that prideless assertion: I am! I exist! I'm alive, I'm called so-and-so, I'm European! A hopeless affirmation, in fact, since when you need to prove the obvious, it is by no means obvious.

★

The process of liberation is never innocent. It starts out from an ideology and an idealist movement in history. It tends always towards a reduction of the fundamental ambivalence of Good and Evil. Good or bad, the fact of being 'liberated' absolves us of an original evil. There is an element of simplification and transparency, of the elimination of the dark continent, the dark side, the accursed share, and the coming of the reign of value: all these things are present in the Rousseauist concept of a happy destiny, a natural vocation, a 'liberation'.

Not to be free is immoral, and liberation is both baptism and salvation, the true democratic sacrament.

Now, this is a utopian model. You cannot liberate Good without liberating Evil, and the ambivalence is definitive. The historical advance of the forces of Evil undoubtedly proceeds even more rapidly than that of the forces of Good. Another problematic consequence: as soon as they are liberated, things begin to float – money in speculation, sex in the lack of defined sexual boundaries, production in senseless overproduction, time in the undecidable calculation of origins. Once they are liberated, things take both an uncertain and an exponential turn. An uncontrollable ratcheting-up (e.g. nuclear power) and, at the same time, the beginning of the countdown: as soon as there is accounting, a calculation of value and accumulation, there is the prospect of exhaustion. Liberation leads always to a critical threshold beyond which its effects are reversed.

Liberty has succumbed to its perverse effect: liberation. In its accepted philosophical sense, liberty is an idea and, by fulfilling it, we have lost it. More or less the same thing happened with desire which faded as an ideal at the same time. Thus liberty, by its own logic, died a natural death, abolished in our profoundest imagination. But it still has to die an unnatural, ignoble one, dragged in effigy through all the discourses which stand in for it – including the discourse of human rights, and more generally all the forms which have replaced existence with the right to existence, difference with the right to difference, desire with the right to desire – and, finally, liberty with the right to be what one is and to want what one wants, which is its derisory form. Liberty thus shares the fate of all these defunct values, exhumed and resuscitated by the work of mourning – nostalgic and melancholic values which the system puts back in circulation as an additional 'moral dimension'.

One can understand why the individual wants one thing only: to be rid of it. 'Being nothing is intoxicating, and the will is a bucket you knocked over in the yard, with a lazy flick of the foot, as you went by' (Pessoa).

This paradoxical movement may extend as far as the rejection of this unconditional liberty. The utopia of liberty, once realized, is no longer a utopia, and it is earlier forms, past forms, enslaved forms, which gradually become once again a utopia.

Omar Khayyam: 'Rather one freeman bind with chains of love/Than set a thousand prisoned captives free.'

Let us be clear about this: we are not speaking of the utopia of a historically defunct form of master and slave, but that of a linkage, a concatenation of forms, of a subjection to the cycle of becoming, to the rule of metamorphoses. Not a personal subjection of the slave, but the subjection of words one to another in language. The necessity of a form is of this order: words are not 'free', and it is certainly not the task of writing to 'liberate' them. On the contrary, writing binds them together, links them in 'chains', but they are linked together with 'chains of love'. The only thing they are to be liberated from is, possibly, their meaning – so that they may form a more secret concatenation.

The Hero does not 'liberate' events or historical forces, nor does he construct a history. He connects, concatenates the figures of myth and legend; that is why neither Revolution nor Democracy needs heroes. The Poet does not 'liberate' words according to their meaning. He binds them together in accordance with the figures of the language; this is why the Republic has no need of poets. The Madman and the Idiot do not 'liberate' drives or lift repression. They rediscover the secret concatenation of the figures of madness – which is closer to an archaic metamorphosis or an otherworldly curse than to desire and the unconscious.

More generally, forms are not liberated; only forces are liberated. The world of forces, of values, and even of ideas – the entire world of liberation – is the world of progress and competitive striving. Forms, for their part, do not surpass each other: there is movement from one form to another, and this play of forms is tragic and sacrificial; whereas relations of force, conflicts of values and ideology, are merely dramatic and conflictual. All the figures of modernity, of liberation, are utopian: theirs is a dream of an ideal non-place. Forms, for their part – the forms of art, for example – are not inspired by utopianism: they do not dream of surpassing themselves towards some other end; they are, in themselves, the non-place.

In any case, to be liberated you have first to have been a slave. And to have been a slave, you have to have not been sacrificed (only the prisoners who were not sacrificed became slaves). Something of this exemption from sacrifice and something of the consequent servility persists in 'liberated' man, particularly in today's servility – not the servility which precedes liberation, but the servility which succeeds it. Servility of the second kind: servility without a master.

In ancient society, there was the master and the slave. Later came the lord and the serf. Later still, the capitalist and the wage-labourer. There is a servitude particular to each of these stages: you know who is the master, who the slave. It is all different now. The master has disappeared. Only the serfs and servility remain. Now, what is a slave without a master? A person who has devoured his master and internalized him, to the point of becoming his own master. He has not killed him in order to become master (that is Revolution); he has absorbed him while remaining a slave – indeed, more slavish than a slave, more servile than a serf: his own serf. The final stage of his servility which, from one regression to another, eventually reaches back to the point of sacrifice. Except that no one any longer does him the honour of sacrificing him, and he is forced, in despair, to sacrifice himself to himself and his own will. Our service-based society is a serf-based society, a society of individuals rendered servile for their own use, slaves to their own functions and performance – perfectly emancipated, perfectly servile.

If the problem of freedom can no longer be posed, then we have to think up an original way of not posing it – or of going beyond it. What is there beyond freedom? The same alternative faces us here as when we ask about the end: what is there beyond the end?

The equivalent in the register of freedom of what occurs in jokes or poetic language (in which words are not free to be exchanged for others, nor exchanged for their meaning, but exchanged as they have, in themselves, been changed by the grace of language) is that people, above and beyond their own wills, are what they are; are the direct coming-to-pass of what they are and what they do – at least in their 'poetic' moments, when they are not representing anything – especially not themselves as subjects. The rest – the rhetoric of will, responsibility and freedom, the image-playback of our whole moral philosophy – is all very well for the disenchanted consciousness of the alienated subject, the subject who is 'liberated' because they no longer know what do with him as a slave, he himself not knowing what to do with his freedom.

It is, in fact, a highly relative freedom, this freedom to become responsible, as a subject, for the objective conditions of one's own life. As long as I am subject to objective conditions, I am still an object, I am not wholly free – I have to be freed from that freedom itself. And this is possible only in play, in that more subtle freedom of play, the arbitrary rules of which paradoxically free me, whereas in reality I am kept in chains by my own will.

The Dice Man

One may, thus, envisage submitting to an arbitrary set of rules, as in Luke Rhinehart's *The Dice Man*. Creating a micro-situation governed by fate, so that the problem of the will no longer arises. One day the hero decides to gamble his life on the throw of a dice. From that point on, the dice alone will decide whether he is, for example, to seduce a particular woman, break with a friend, go off to India, do nothing and simply take a holiday, or commit suicide.

> Chance is the most ancient divinity of the world, and behold, I come to deliver all things from their bondage under Purpose. . . . The mind is in bondage to Purpose and Will, but I shall free it to Divine Accident and Prankishness. . . .

> What if [the sense of self] represents a psychological appendix: a useless anachronistic pain in the side? – or, like the mastodon's huge tusks: a heavy, useless and ultimately self-destructive burden? What if the sense of being someone represents an evolutionary error as disastrous to the further development of a more complex creature as was the shell for snails or turtles?

Is not thought, consciousness itself, an appendix, an aberration, a hypertelic excrescence, a luxurious but lethal dysfunction, which contravenes the whole of evolution by suddenly becoming aware of it – paralysed by its own image?

There is, then, something fundamental at stake in this existential throw of the dice: it means no longer having any illusions about one's own will; it means going beyond this and opening up to an objective randomness which might be seen as the randomness of the world itself. It is, then, a way of transferring one's will, of delegating power.

Dice as the ultimate projection of an impersonal will, of a decision taken elsewhere. The sign – in negative, so to speak – that someone is looking after you, that you are not left merely to your own devices, that there is otherness somewhere. As seen in so many other forms in the past: the stars, a chicken's entrails, the flight of birds. For good or ill, our fate is decided elsewhere.

However, a kind of paradox distorts things from the outset: the decision to surrender to chance is not taken by chance. In this sense, a throw of the dice – countless throws of the dice – will never abolish the initial determination. Unless that resolve to rely on chance is the product of an even more subtle form of chance. . . . Moreover, the options (each throw of the die provides six options) have to be set down in advance by the person gambling his fate. But what governs the selection of possible destinies? Is it absolute chance? Certainly not. At the moment the subject schedules his options, what is involved is neither pure, objective chance nor a determined will, but, in a sense, a subjective chance, steered by the unconscious wishes of the subject: seduction, rape, murder, orgy or, on the other hand, love, security, happiness, sacrifice. However this may be, just as nothing can come out of a computer which hasn't been programmed in, nothing can come from the dice which hasn't already been programmed mentally. And if the aim is to liberate oneself from any will of one's own, then one is deluded in the attempt. The whole undertaking is an illusion, and recourse to the dice seems pointless if it leads back only to the banal contingency of desire.

Clearly, objective chance is merely an illusion, a utopian dream. The *Dé-cision* (to make a French pun which sums up the whole of Rhinehart's book) is never as arbitrary as we think (just as automatic writing is never truly automatic), and chance never lies in the choice we make from among chance events. Unless, that is, you purely and simply give in to what happens to you – but even then we know that, in the end, nothing happens to you by accident.

The whole book is proof *a contrario* that it is impossible to opt for chance, impossible to live by a rigorous deregulation of the will, but equally impossible to opt for the will, which, as we know, is self-deluding. In fact, chance does not exist. And neither does the will. The rules governing our lives are to be found elsewhere.

There is, moreover, a strange contradiction between the exercise of the will and the exercise of freedom. It's always nice to take a decision – and equally nice to put one off. You have to know how to play with a decision. The decision is the key thing – what you decide will work out one way or another, whatever you do. Now, every decision taken is a double-edged sword. Adopting a decision immediately turns it into a prohibition: it becomes something not to be transgressed. There is then no difference between it being your decision or someone else's. To decide 'sovereignly', you have to be able to determine how to proceed in relation to your own decision, to reconsider it freely, as though it were in fact someone else's.

To be able to disobey moral rules and laws, to be able to disobey others, is a mark of freedom. But the ability to disobey oneself marks the highest stage of freedom. Obeying one's own will is an even worse vice than being enslaved to one's passions. It is certainly worse than enslavement to the will of others. And it is, indeed, those who submit themselves mercilessly to their own decisions who fill the greater part of the authoritarian ranks, alleging sacrifice on their own part to impose even greater sacrifices on others.

Each stage of servitude is both more subtle and worse than the one which precedes it. Involuntary servitude, the servitude of the slave, is overt violence. Voluntary servitude is a violence consented to: a freedom to will, but not the will to be free. Last comes voluntary self-servitude or enslavement to one's own will: the individual possesses the faculty to will, but is no longer free in respect of it. He is the automatic agent of that faculty. He is the serf to no master but himself.

Although it purports to be rid of the will, the self and desire, Rhinehart's fable still pays them far too much respect. The will is presented as a barrier which has to be overcome for total liberation of the self, of all conceivable selves, to be possible. This is still a very naive vision of a natural order of the will, which is to be transcended in the supernatural order of chance. It is a vision of a desire limited by the law, but with chance able to unlock its possibilities. It would seem that in order to break down the barrier of the will, one has to see it as already broken down – to see our most ordinary decisions as already in themselves random in nature, and bearing only a superficial relation to the subject and his will.

Chance is already present everywhere. There is no need to produce it through the simulacrum of an imposed rule. Arbitrariness lies not in choosing chance, but in the unpredictable as it exists, in the relation to others as they are, in the unforeseen events of the world and its appearances. Raw existence is, in the end, more improbable than the improbability of dice, and the oblique line of destiny runs through that existence without either our will or a higher will being involved.

The Other makes its appearance, come what may. It is the Other which, at every moment, creates the dividing line. At every moment, without any forcing – or willing – things fall one side or other of that line. The rules of the way of the world are already laid down. Radical absence of will is to be found in the immanent disorder of the real world. The dice-life and its willed *dé-viance* (to offer another French pun) is superfluous. In this sense, constructing an artificial destiny with dice operates almost to protect you against the unpredictable fatefulness of the world as it is.

It is the will to chance which is misguided and which, in the end, torpedoes the whole undertaking in a systematic staging of events. One can understand Rhinehart's dream of being the agent of a secret rule, the protagonist of an order of Evil or a universal disorder through glorifying chance and staging chance events. But when all is said and done, neither he nor the seducer of *Les Liaisons dangereuses*, nor Sade's criminal can take responsibility for the definitively impersonal character of their acts. We are neither preordained criminals nor preordained victims, and we cannot choose our fate.

Programming the deregulation of life is impossible; the rule of chance is impossible, as is any strategy of fate or intentional seduction: it is a contradiction in terms. 'Historical necessity is merely a necessity *a fresca* (improvised, projected retrospectively on to the event), and it is impossible to predict an event with mathematical certainty before it has actually happened. God himself could not predict it, and the more He was God, the less it would be possible' (Schnitzler). Hence the illusory nature of the dice, with surprise, the unforeseeable, as the only possibility. 'He who truly knows how to live will appreciate the little surprises which always await him in the least significant event.'

In the end, Rhinehart recognizes that everyone else lives multiple lives which are the product of chance too, even if they do not know it and spend their lives trying to deny it. So, the establishment of a purely random universe (if such a thing were possible) would not in the least change the world as it currently exists. This was already the hypothesis where the virtual economy – of free-floating capital and pure speculation – is concerned. Once it has been virtually achieved and become perfect in itself, that speculative, orbital sphere – like the sphere of the networks and information – no longer affects the 'real' world, which continues to run its course on a parallel trajectory. We might say the same of God Himself, chance being merely a hypostasis of God. Whether God exists or not changes nothing. That is why proofs of the existence of God, like the possible verification of chance, are ultimately pointless. Naturally, 'a throw of the dice will never abolish chance',[1] since chance does not, in the end, exist, and another throw of the dice simply adds to the uncertainty of the world as it is. We might similarly say that the proof that the world is materialist in essence will not abolish the existence of God since, fundamentally, that existence does not matter one way or the other, is unverifiable, and is just another name for the course of things.

The idea of Chance is, then, supererogatory (it introduces an abstract, redundant dimension). As for its basic philosophy, it is redhibitory (it contains an unseen defect which presents a radical obstacle). Thus, as the idea works itself out, the action of the novel goes downhill. Admittedly, this philosophy of a deliverance from the Self, of a freedom unfettered by anything but self-imposed rules, absolves the gamer of any responsibility, and confers much greater immunity on him than any moral or political freedom. And in the Protean (anti-Promethean) universe in which everyone changes role randomly, all the anxieties and inhibitions which go with social and psychological identity are relaxed. This is why the Babylonians in Borges's fable had chosen to entrust their fate to the Lottery, preferring that uncertainty to the torments of individual responsibility and free will.

And yet the dream of shattering the identitary ego in order to embrace plural destinies is a naive superstition. Fundamentally, it is the same as the superstitious

---

1. 'Un coup de dés jamais n'abolira le hasard', the title of one of Mallarmé's best-known texts.

belief in virtual networks and computer games, with their ideal of the dispersion of the individual 'spectrum' (Marc Guillaume). Does the fact that the dice tell me to seduce a particular woman induce in me a desire for that woman? (Objection: if I selected her as an option, then perhaps I already desired her. But where, then, is the need to involve the dice and to force myself to obey my own desire?) Does the fact that the networks put me in touch with a particular partner, or open up some new possibility, liberate other egos within me?

Not at all. To project one's ego absolutely anywhere, to embark upon interactivity with simply anyone, is not to become other. It is, in fact, the very opposite. The Other and otherness come into play only in a dual relationship, never in a multiple or plural one. Only in duality are the sexes *fatal* to each other. In multiple relations they are merely mirrors of each other, and interlocking self-refractions. If chance means that the combinations are infinite in number, and everything is possible, that is quite the opposite of Destiny.

This is where the novel degenerates, too. For the spectre of existence governed by the dice in this way ends in banal role-play and in a collective psychodrama increasingly obsessed with sex and orgies.

> He becomes ecstatic. He experiences the transfer of control from an illusory self to the dice as a conversion or as salvation. . . . In all these cases the ego-control game is abandoned and the student surrenders to a force which is experienced as being outside himself;

and, at the same time: 'Suddenly I was free of all my hangups about raping little girls.'

In the drive 'liberated' by chance, it is the unmotivated character of desire which wins out, not the unmotivated character of the dice game. The divine uncertainty of gambling becomes once again the instrument of desire, and Chance, previously referred to as divine accident and divine prankishness, becomes once again the vulgar instrument of obscure wishes.

To this is added the other perversion – in a sense, the logical conclusion to this *trompe-l'œil* deregulation – the perversion of a categorical immoral imperative: elevating dice and Chance into a universal principle, if not indeed a systematic 'dice-therapy', with its 'Centers for Experiments in Totally Random Environments'. This takes us into the worst kind of utopia – an insider raving,[2] which slides automatically into cultish practices with the violence characteristic of that type of organization, where arbitrariness figures no longer as a function of chance, but as arbitrary power.

The magnificent failure of a defiance of any will of one's own, of an anarchistic defiance of all forms of power (including the power all exert on themselves through that same will). Paradoxically, devolving power to the rolling dice – the attempt to disappropriate the will – ends up resembling the venture of that other anarchist, Stirner, who, in *Der Einzige und sein Eigenthum*, aims for total appropriation and unconditional hegemony of the Ego – where the most liberatory principle ends in the most commonplace tyranny. The unhappy fate of many radical utopias, haunted by their redhibitory defects.

Yet the idea of a society governed by chance, as in Borges's 'Lottery in Babylon' or Rhinehart's *Dice Man*, is in some sense an idea of an absolute democracy, since it resolves the inequality of objective conditions into an equality of opportunity with respect to a set of rules. Democracy is, of course, based on equality before the law,

2. 'délire d'initiés' - a pun on 'délit d'initiés': insider trading.

but that is never as radical as equality before the rule. And it is, indeed, this dream of a radical democracy which haunts the imaginations of all gamblers, and makes all forms of gaming a fantastic attraction in all ages, particularly for the middle and working classes, as a refuge for their thwarted demand for 'social' democracy. It is the site of 'luck', the only non-place where good and bad are not distributed in the same way, and, even in its most impoverished forms, it is the only sumptuary activity – that of a sovereign freedom ignorant of the material conditions of its exercise. The site of a supernatural freedom which bears no relation to 'natural' freedom, and has about it more an immediate collusion with the world. Now, the whole pleasure comes from this. Gaming does not liberate us from constraints (since we accept the far stricter constraint of the rules), but it delivers us from freedom. We lose freedom if we live it merely as reality. The miracle of gaming is to make us live our freedom not as reality but as illusion – a higher illusion, an aristocratic challenge to reality. For reality is democratic, and illusion is aristocratic.

D for Double Life[1]

Another solution to the impossible exchange of one's life is to exchange it for a double life.

This was the solution chosen by Romans, the central character in a criminal trial of the 1990s. Not daring to admit to his family that he had failed his medical examinations, he set up a complete parallel life, a pseudo-career in medicine, supporting his family by a variety of financial ploys until one day he massacred them all, parents, wife and children – mysteriously sparing only his mistress, and that at the last moment.

Why the massacre? On the verge of being unmasked, he could not stand the idea of those who had believed in him ceasing to do so. They simply could not be allowed to discover the truth. There was only one solution: they had to be killed. Suicide would not have kept the deception from his family. His response was logical: he spared them the shame of knowing.

1. In French, the letter 'd' is a homophone of 'dés' (phonetic: [de]) meaning dice.

There is another possible hypothesis, which does not exclude the first: every crime asks secretly to be discovered. Only this time the simulation worked too well, and he blamed them for not having managed to unmask him, for not having been able, over a lifetime, to see through him, and for having let him sink deeper into his deception and trickery, turning him into a veritable simulating machine. This same logic accounts for the mistress being spared, because she had ceased to be a blind accomplice. Indeed, he had taken this woman as his mistress towards the end solely to break the spell, to end the dramatic servitude to his double role. A real crime would at last allow him to own up to his responsibility. This is the opposite pattern from that of the usual criminal, who logically eliminates those who can unmask him. And this is what the judicial system held against him, with due psychological logic: 'You do not destroy those you love [he says he continued to feel affection for them even as he was committing the crime and afterwards]. At worst, you commit suicide.' They cannot believe that, in doing away with his family, his aim was to save them from total disappointment. Yet the logic is watertight: if they had not trusted him so much, he would not have killed them.

Romans is an unprepossessing, melodramatic character, with no profound duplicity in him. In no way was he criminal material. He embarked upon his double life spontaneously, without premeditation, and lived it the way others live a single life. In a way, it was his family and friends who became his double life, and by doing away with them, he recovered a reality and an identity. They are indeed much more present to him now as a forlorn criminal (with the distraught memory of his father he displayed at the trial) than they were in their lifetimes. Or – looked at another way – he sacrificed his real life to his parallel life, in accordance with the rule that there is not enough room for both the real and its double.

At all events, what happened was tantamount to a crime of jealousy. He was jealous of his own image in their eyes. That image had to remain intact for them, and since he did what he did, it will have remained so until death. This is the very logic of the crime of passion: if you cannot have the object, then it must be got rid of once and for all; it must disappear.

The peculiar feature of this case is that it gives rise to a radical suspicion: what if every 'normal' existence concealed a successful simulation? Not a perverse or romantic one, but a simulation that was perfectly banal – a parallel existence which did not intersect with the other (from time to time, however, the parallel lines meet, and catastrophe ensues). This opens up amazing possibilities: we might be surrounded by pathological liars and know nothing of it, since there is no way to tell a 'normal' man from an entirely unremarkable impostor, going around freely beneath a conventional exterior (like those spies who are 'sleepers' in foreign countries until one day they are 'activated'). Seen from this angle, the most insignif-icant of our fellow citizens becomes both suspect and seductive. Everyone becomes virtually capable of massacring their family to prevent the truth getting out. Everything becomes possible as soon as one life may conceal another. There is no need to change your life – all you need is to have two.

Viewed from this suspicious angle, it gradually dawns that you have only to look at the political and social world to see that it is made up of countless parallel, 'rigged' careers, of speculation and crookery which is never denounced, of perfectly impenetrable insider deals, of mystifications we shall never see unmasked. But these impostures and double dealings normally disappear into the system itself, whereas for Romans – a minor extra in his own psychodrama – it ended in a shoot-out with reality.

What the judicial system condemned in the person of Romans was this fantas-tic suspicion he cast on personal identity, and hence on the whole of the social order. For this he clearly deserves to be locked away indefinitely.

Besides, he never offended against morality, only against reality – which is much more serious. When he claims that he cannot explain how the simulation was maintained, he is 'sincere', since the simulation was from the outset produced by the silent collusion of others. Simulation is like a prophecy which, by being repeated, becomes self-fulfilling.

It needs no initial motive; its motive force arises out of the process itself, without any relation of cause and effect. This is why it is absurd to quiz Romans on his motives, or to make him confess to anything whatever. One is responsible only in respect of *causes*, whereas he can answer only for the fateful sequence of events, the irresistible concatenation of *effects* (it doesn't make any sense, but it works). The perfect crime is the crime with no ulterior motive; the one which simply follows out a train of thought.

Romans's solution was an extreme one. He does not play at multiple lives, as Luke Rhinehart's hero does, and he does not, strictly speaking, 'act' a character. He haunts his own life as though it were another's; he practises a kind of radical exoticism, of lethal severance from the world.

There are other, more temperate forms of exoticism, of minimal strategies of self-duplication. One such is acting itself, as presented in Diderot's *Paradox of the Actor* or in Brecht's *Verfremdungseffekt*, conceptions far removed from any compulsion to identify psychologically with the character, or from that general frenzied empathy which holds sway today in the theatre.

There is in the actor, in the best of cases, a form of distance which sees to it that roles and images do not intermingle. He has to maintain the strangeness of the actor's other – the character – on pain of frittering away the power of the stage into theatrical grandstanding. He has to preserve the differential of illusion, the differential of otherness, in order to safeguard the energy specific to the stage. To do so, he has basically to be a snob – has to 'affect' his role rather than personify it, implicitly signifying: 'This is not me; I have nothing to do with this'. Snobbery lies in resisting the easy solution of identifying with anything whatever, anyone whatever, as our whole psychological conformism invites us to. If we are to end up being the exotics of our own lives (as we all are), we may as well cultivate radical exoticism.

Should we take the view that this distance, this offhandedness, towards our own being is an exception? Or has it not always been there? Our society has, in fact, become performance-orientated and operational in all its aspects, but it does not believe in these things – though most of the time it does not realize that it does not believe in them. We are unwitting agnostics; we live by this affectation – the product of a profound incredulity – which consists in doing more and doing too much. There is in this a snobbery of the operational, a neurosis of performance which we collectively act out, and which protects us from a bestial condition or, in other words, from pure functionality (see Kojève and his alternative of Japanese snobbery or American animality). This is why these 'discontents of civilization' are never so serious as they are said to be, for we secretly play-act technology and performance, play-act information and efficiency. We set the distance to the 'reality', the hyperreality, of our world, as we do that of a photographic lens. It is set at maximum zoom with a stereoscopic range of effects, but we ourselves are not taken in by these. Yet we enjoy the effect of enlargement and the dizzying sense of simulation and, precisely because we do not believe in it, we are capable of going much further with the operational scenario than we would be if we did.

This is, doubtless, the secret of Japanese technology, of that heroic affectation, that functional heroism of the Empire of the Sun. But even in the West, something of this free-and-easy attitude to values, accompanied by an intensification of practices, shows through. Business looks more and more like a performative game, with maximum energy being put into the – no longer orthodox, but paradoxical –

scenario of the enterprise. It is an almost suicidal energy that is vested in this way in the disillusioned scenario of all-out growth and speculation. But it is, above all, an energy released by a scaling down of the stakes, a collapse of goals and constraints.

This is, more or less, the opposite of the double bind: there is no longer any contradictory tension on either side, with regard either to ends or to means – performance alone counts: an overactivity de-cathected and de-ideologized on the basis of fundamental lack of belief in its own essence; an overactivity both *désinvolte* and, literally, disinvolved. The modern entrepreneur (and we are all entrepreneurs) is agnostic. (The worker did not believe in what he was doing either, but for other reasons!)

Yet is there not, on the margins of this de-cathexis, this transparency, this casualness – at the end of this general affectation – another form of psychosis and melancholia lying in wait for us?

At any rate, this dialectic of actor and character is a thing of the past – the dialectic we find in the faces, costumes and gestures of 1940s and 1950s cinema, a period still dominated, even in daily life, by the theatricality of characters and roles. In metaphysical terms, this was the world of Sartre's waiter – the waiter who spoke like a waiter, saw himself as a waiter, and so on. Today, that entire social and psychological theatre, that entire existential psychodrama, has been swept away by the directive, interactive behaviour of a society without actors (and as this has happened, we have rediscovered a kind of poetry in the old state of affairs, a poetry underscored in the cinema by black-and-white).

May '68 was still faithful in its gestures and speech to that cultural rhetoric (which in no way detracts from the symbolic violence of the event). Our age, however, is no longer capable of providing a stage and actors. We shall not even seem faintly ridiculous to those who come after us, in the way 1950s characters do to us. We have thrown off that old existential garb. We are defrocked – divested of ideology, of the class struggle, of history. We are active, interactive individuals, who no longer tell each other (hi)stories, no longer see ourselves as waiters. That 'Belle Époque' was the era of bad conscience and bad faith – Sartre grasped its historical torment most accurately – and the moving shadows of the cinema of that age express marvellously well the – already banal – post-Romantic death throes of subjectivity, all the nuances of the obsolete Character, and the aporias of freedom.

Who cares about freedom, bad faith and authenticity today? The mask has fallen, leaving behind the insignificant self-evidence of the Real, the *écriture automatique* of the Virtual. Roles have been eclipsed, and with them the specific hysteria of that 'Belle Époque', the hysteria of the décor and the scene, the rhetoric of an age still grappling with the mirror stage of modernity and not yet doomed to the definitive screen stage – the stage of a cold epilepsy and an overcharged inertia, in which the old golden triangle of the real, the symbolic and the imaginary is no longer valid, no longer quoted on the mental stock exchange of values.

The Flow of Change
The Cycle of Becoming
The Divide of Destiny

The Flow of Change
The Cycle of Becoming

Plural identities, double lives, objective chance or variable-geometry destinies – all this seems very much like the invention of artificial, substitute fates. Sex, genes, networks, desires and partners – everything now falls within the ambit of change and exchange. Destiny, pain – everything is becoming optional. Death itself is an option. The very sign of birth, your astrological sign, will one day be optionally available in a future Zodiacal Surgery Institute, where, under certain conditions, you will be able to change your birth sign the way you can change your face today.

All these options are ultimately mere variants of the impossible exchange of one's own life. The very opposite of a destiny. The very opposite of that pre-eminent figure of destiny that is the Eternal Return, the marvellous possibility of which assumes that things are caught up in a necessary, fated succession which exceeds their control. Nothing of the kind exists today, things being caught up, as they are, in a contiguity running off to infinity. The Eternal Return is now the return of the infinitely small, the fractal – the repetition of a microscopic, inhuman scale. It is no longer the exalting of a will, the sovereign affirmation of a Becoming and its consecration in an immutable sign, but the viral recurrence of micro-processes — a recurrence which is itself ineluctable, but which no sign conveys to the imagination. These processes weigh down on us like an exorbitant but meaningless burden — there is suspense, but no destiny. The fateful against the fractal, change against becoming.

> The mutual antagonism of passions, the duality, trinity, plurality of 'souls in a single breast': very unhealthy; inner ruin; destructive; betraying and intensifying an inner conflict and anarchism, unless one passion eventually becomes master. . . . The most interesting people belong in this category, the chameleons; they are not in contradiction with themselves . . . but they have no development — their various states lie side by side, even if they are separated up to seven times. They change, but they do not *become*. (Nietzsche)

In plurality, multiplicity, a being merely exchanges itself for itself or for one of its many avatars. It produces metastases; it does not metamorphose. 'The intensity of a consuming passion metamorphoses a unity — chameleons, for their part, show no contradictory tension; they merely provide its simulacrum.' Destiny, becoming and otherness are diffracted into the perpetual exchanging of selves, into the 'spectrum of identities' (Marc Guillaume). The physical multiplicity of the colours of the spectrum, the virtual spectrum of all the technical possibilities of individuation, the changeability of the chameleon: a single pattern — that of exchange along a spectrum. Interactivity, mobility, virtuality: a gigantic enterprise of simulation and a parody of becoming.

Ideas, too, change and multiply: their succession forms part of a history of ideas, and of their hypothetical finality. But in another dimension, the dimension of destiny and becoming (that precise place where thought 'becomes'), there is only ever a single idea: the master hypothesis, equivalent to the master passion of which

Nietzsche speaks. For him, it was the idea of the Eternal Return, the idea of a singularity linked to integral becoming and the Eternal Return.

The master passion, like the master hypothesis, delivers us from all the others, delivers us from that plurality, that frenzied exchange of modes of thought and modes of existence which is merely the caricature and simulacrum of becoming.

In terms of ideas, anything is possible – what is needed is a master hypothesis.

In terms of desire, anything is possible – what is needed is a master passion.

In terms of ends and purposes, anything is possible – what is needed is a predestination and a destiny.

In terms of change, anything is possible – what is needed is a metamorphosis and a becoming.

In terms of otherness, anything is possible (conviviality, instant communication, networks) – what is needed is a dual, antagonistic and irreducible form.

Against this assumption into generalized exchange, this movement of convergence towards the Single and the Universal: the dual form, irrevocable divergence. Against all that is striving to reconcile the antagonistic terms: maintain impossible exchange, play on the very impossibility of that exchange, play on that tension and that dual form, which nothing escapes, but everything opposes.

At all events, this duality governs us. Each individual life unfolds on two levels, in two dimensions – history and destiny – which coincide only exceptionally. Each life has its history, the history of its successive events, its twists and turns – but elsewhere, in another dimension, there is only one form, that of the absolute becoming of the same situation, which occurs for everyone in the form of an Eternal Return. The form of destiny, which Nietzsche also calls 'character', to distinguish it from any psychology of the ego and its successive changes.

The Divide of Destiny

Somewhere in Colorado there is a demarcation line where the waters part – the so-called Continental Divide – some running off to the Atlantic, the rest to the Pacific. It is a line almost as imaginary as the one separating the past from the future – that line we call the present. And the two dimensions of time themselves run off and vanish into oceanic depths of their own. The instant, that dividing line, is a line of destiny: past and future part there, never to meet again. And existence is merely this ever-greater divergence of past and future, until death reunites the two in an absolute present.

In man, it is thoughts which divide – the 'mental divide'. Like the continental waters, they run off unpredictably in opposite directions, and often those which were closest together will end up furthest apart.

It is along this same imaginary line that men and women, good and evil, signs and languages divide. At the origin there is always this demarcation line which creates something more than a difference: a definitive divergence. Not only do things separate, but, like constellations of signs or the constellations in space, they continue to move apart endlessly. Just as the waters, which come from the same sky, divide, so human destinies, coming from the same primal scene, take a different course. On either side of an imaginary line of will, each decision creates two slopes, where life runs off in opposite directions – each fraction moving irremediably away from the other.

But the same sign which presides over the separation of things is the very sign which reunites them. For division can indicate a dividing into separate parts or into shares – a sharing. On either side of the dividing line, things remain inseparable none the less, and those things which diverge the most none the less come together again.

We have all had, on one or more occasions, a rendezvous with death, even if it was not in Samarkand. That rendezvous is no different from any other encounter of virtually zero probability. Every strange coincidence has a probability virtually equal to zero. Every conjunction is a gamble on causal relations – a 'probing of the etiological mystery of random conjunctures', as Nabokov would say.

> There are always at least two occasions when two persons, unwittingly, almost met. Each time destiny seems to have prepared this meeting with the greatest care, attending first to one possibility, then another, ordering the tiniest detail and leaving nothing to chance. But each time some tiny, unattended eventuality intervenes to prevent the coming together, and the two lives diverge once again at a greater rate. . . . But destiny is much too persistent to allow itself to be put off by a failure. It arrives at its ends, by such subtle machinations that not even a click is heard when at last the two persons are brought together.

As time goes by, however, destiny wearies and no longer bothers to contrive these coincidences: this is one's lot in old age, when they become increasingly rare, till the coming of death, which by that time is merely the arrival of an automatic term.

So long as this destiny is at work, the probability of any event, even if it has not taken place, is never exhausted. And it is this, this actual grace of coincidences – and never a chain of causality – which makes the event of a life. When this grace is lacking, history grows old and repetitious, all possibilities are fused, and life slips back into an undifferentiated vegetal or animal state.

We can recall moments in the past when we had equal chances of living or dying – in a car crash, for example. Naturally, the person talking about it has chosen to survive, but, at the same time, the other has chosen death. Every time someone finds himself at a crossroads of this kind, he has two worlds before him. One loses all reality, because he dies there; the other remains real, because he survives. He abandons the world in which he is now only dead, and settles into the one in which he is still alive. There is, then, a life in which he is alive, and another in which he is dead. The bifurcation of the two, linked to a particular contingent detail, is sometimes so subtle that one cannot but believe that the fateful event is continuing its course elsewhere. (And indeed, it often appears in dreams, in which you relive it to the end.) This alternative is not, then, an entirely phantom one; it exists in the mind, and leads a parallel existence. We cannot speak of the unconscious here, since neither repression nor the return of the repressed is involved. It is merely that two units have separated and, though they are increasingly distant (my current life is increasingly different from the one which began for the virtual dead man at that moment), they are indivisible.

It is the same with each decisive moment, both with birth and with death. Just as the virtual dead man that I am continues on his way on the other side, carries on with his existence which runs just beneath the surface of mine, birth is that dividing line where on the one side I exist as myself, but on the other I begin, at the same moment, to exist as other. Such is the form of alterity, and I cannot conceive of myself not having this secret alterity, the product of both separation and inseparability.

That which has separated definitively – for example, the I from the non-I at birth – continues none the less to run along another line. These lines, or these parallel lives, meet only in death. But at certain moments, you can jump from one to the other, cross one of these other lives. Destiny dooms us to a personal death, but something of this multiple predestination remains. Alterity is a trace of these crossings, which provide one of the grids of becoming: becoming-animal, becoming-plant, becoming-woman – crossing the demarcation line between the sexes and the species. It is the same with words in language, which remains the model of becoming. Words do not respect the limits of meaning; they continually mingle with parallel significations.

At the point where this irreversible separation takes place – between the animate and the inanimate, the sexed and the unsexed – emerges the equally irresistible denial of this separation. The living will retain a nostalgia for the inanimate, the sexed a nostalgia for the unsexed and the sexes a nostalgia for each other. Thought will retain a nostalgia for unintelligent matter, or for the beasts which neither speak nor think.

The two drives are equally violent: the drive for liberation – the breaking away of life, sex and thought – and the sense of remorse, of repentance for that break. Destiny lies on each side, but it is more precisely present at the points where they intersect most violently.

Thus each existence is the product of a double declension. It is in this sense that it is a dual, not an individual, form. We are not free to exist just on the side of our ego, our identity, or just on that of the so-called real world. We are wholly the products of this relation of adversity, this twin complicity. Destiny is divided, like thought, which comes to us from the other. Each is the destiny of the other. There is no individual destiny.

But if I am inseparable from the other, from all the others I almost became, then all destinies are linked, and no one can claim to have his own life or his own thought. Being is a linked succession of forms, and to speak of one's own will makes no sense. Existence is 'allotted' to us, and all forms of transference are possible, on the basis of a symbolic apportionment from which all other cultures have derived their basic rule. Neither existence nor the world belongs to us; they are allotted to us in a reciprocal arrangement which is the golden rule. In this ideal form, we can say, literally, that it is the world which thinks us, the other which thinks us, the object which thinks us. Whether it be intelligence, power or seduction, everything comes to us from elsewhere, from this dual, parallel concatenation. This – which was the secret of cultures that have now disappeared – runs counter to our modern determination to think the world objectively, unilaterally, without a hint of reciprocity. Without doubt, nothing has changed fundamentally, and even with us moderns, it is still the world which thinks us. The difference is that today we think the opposite.

No doubt everyone is actually present with their wills and their desires, but secretly their decisions and thoughts come to them from elsewhere. And it is in this very strange interaction that their originality lies – their destiny. The destiny we are constantly seeking to escape.

What is the point of willing when, on either side of the imaginary line of the will, both sides of a decision continue to exist in parallel? From time to time, what we did not will interferes with the chosen solution, and triumphs against our will. But it does not do so without a secret assent, since it is still *we* who did not will it. Most often, things just happen and then retrospectively organize themselves into an idea of a plan, into an idea of a will which sanctions the event a posteriori, in the same way as the dream narrative is constructed at the moment of waking.

So Canetti says of vengeance that no purpose is served by wishing for it, since it happens come what may, according to the fundamental rule of reversibility. The point is – above and beyond all the categories of willing, knowing and believing – to discover a parting of destinies and a strategy of otherness, whether in this plurality of collusive, parallel universes or in any form which alters the individual being – which displaces, metabolizes, metamorphoses or captivates him. On this tack, one may, paradoxically, simply let things happen: let the other will, know, decide or desire. This is not a form of defeating desire, but of sidestepping or outwitting it, of ironically investing the other. A more seductive, more effective stratagem than that of the will. A more powerful strategy than that of desire: playing with desire.

In this way, one can offload one's will, one's desire, on to someone else and, in return, become free to take on responsibility for someone else's life. A symbolic circulation of affects and destinies is created, a cycle of alterity – beyond alienation and all the individual psychology in which we are trapped. There is in this symbolic circulation, in this sharing of destinies, the essence of a subtler freedom than the individual liberty to make up one's mind according to one's conscience – a liberty which ultimately we do not know what to do with, and which it is, in fact, better to slough off right away, in order to recover the impersonal concatenation of signs, events, affects and passions.

To all the categories of facticity we can respond, in this way, with mirror strategies: resolving the ambiguity of all these individual functions – willing, believing, knowing – by a straight transference on to the desire or will of another. Something like *a poetic transference of the situation, or a poetic situation of transference.*

The story of the Japanese woman who, unhappy at having known neither love nor pain, hires a geisha, whose lover has just left her, to love and suffer in her place, is a truly wonderful tale. And when the lover returns, the geisha opts to stay with this woman who has chosen her, and on whose behalf she experiences passion. Elective affinity is stronger than the passion of love. Unlike our individual choices, elective affinity is a meeting of two trajectories. In that meeting, you do not choose; you are chosen. And it is in being chosen, being elected in this way, that the greatest pleasure lies – not in the options you take for your own life.

Is it not our constant desire, in the absence of God, to convert this accidental world into something intended for us – an elective form, a magical convergence? And it matters little whether the outcome is good or bad, provided that this fatedness transforms us into strange attractors, which is something we all dream of.

Just because a tile falls off a roof, there isn't necessarily someone underneath it at the right moment: that would be too good to be true. And just because you fall in love with someone, that doesn't mean they will respond automatically to your desire: an automatic wish fulfilment of that kind would be hellish. Yet we feel that everyone somehow dreams of such a fateful conjunction – if not, perhaps, of being the person right underneath the tile. Though even then there may be exhilaration in feeling favoured by ill fortune.

So we find mysterious relief in a succession of accidents or setbacks. One accident is negative. Two is neither one thing nor the other. Three or four in a row is a thrill. We like to see fate rounding on us in this way. It shows that we have become a focal point, that someone 'up there' is taking an interest. It reminds us of the days when the powers of heaven and hell did battle over our souls.

The desire for events to converge is greater than the fear of the event itself – the desire to see causal logic dismantled, a logic which we find deeply repellent, even if we obey the dominant moral imperative and speak in causal terms. We dream of seeing things strung together by a secret logic, entirely independent of our wills.

The radical choice, then, is between the will and an essential determination from elsewhere, between volition and devolution, between a bias towards the will (for it *is* a form of bias) and the bias towards a radical otherness, an impersonal, arbitrary form.

It seems that God Himself, our causal God, the Grand Master of Causes and Effects, has chosen simply to let things happen and has withdrawn, leaving the field to pure chance and indeterminacy, or to pure seduction and general predestination – as we can say, with Baltasar Gracián: keeping man eternally in suspense, and leaving the world to its secret destiny. For Him, this is nothing less than transferring His will to the world (Spinoza), transferring His divine thought to the world, and in the process transferring the responsibility for thinking us to the event of the world – assigning human thought to a space governed by the impersonal thinking of the other, a space where other correlations than our own are in play. This is not a question of relying on chance. Mallarmé's formula, 'A dice throw never will abolish chance', is true from the statistical, mathematical point of view (apart from its poetic value) in that no event can put an end to the succession of events, and no action can definitively determine what follows. But the gambler does not believe in chance. On the contrary, he aspires to abolish it at every throw of the dice. To make a pact with chance is not to speculate on random events, but to attune oneself to the world, to explore its secret connections and concatenations; it is, in a sense, to be initiated. And every win is a sign of the success of that initiation.

This sublime sensation which makes gambling such a heady phenomenon is the sense of a total collusion between the random play of the world and your own gaming, of a reversibility between the world and yourself, of a supernatural consonance between your choice and the choice of an order about which you can do nothing, but which seems somehow to be speaking to you and effortlessly obeying you. At this point, the world takes on total responsibility for the game. The world becomes a player; the player, the gambler becomes a world.

Nothing is accidental any more, since, from the point when the world thinks us, things follow on in a sure progression. Nor is anything intentional, a matter of will, since, in a sense, everything has already been willed. And luck – which is a material thing – is merely the emanation, and sanction, of this collusion. To such a point, indeed, that the gambler can imagine himself in command of the game, since, in this total exchange, there is control on both sides. The gambler then experiences fully, in an intuitive way, the hypothesis of the omnipotence of thought which Freud found evidence of in phantasms and dreams, and primitive peoples saw in the staging of magic rites – a staging which is in no sense an illusory mastery, but a mastery of illusion. 'I am not playing. I am the game.'

This is how Jack, the poker player in Paul Auster's *The Music of Chance*, talks:

That's the feeling I always wait for. It's like a switch turns on inside me, and my whole body starts to hum. Whenever I get that feeling, it means I'm home free. I can coast all the way to the end. . . . Once your luck starts to roll, there's not a damn thing that can stop it. It's like the whole world suddenly falls into place. You're kind of outside your body, and for the rest of the night you sit there watching yourself perform miracles. It doesn't really have anything to do with you anymore. It's out of your control, and as long as you don't think about it too much, you can't make a mistake.

Then there is nothing to rule out the paradoxical hypothesis that it is indeed our thought which governs the world, on condition that we first think that it is the world which thinks us.

'It isn't the man who drinks the tea, it's the tea which drinks the man.'[1]

It isn't you who smoke the pipe, it's the pipe which smokes you.

It's the book which reads me.

It's the TV which watches you.

It's the object which thinks us.

It's the lens which focuses on us.

It's the effect which causes us.

It's language which speaks us.

It's time which wastes us.

It's money which earns us.

It's death which lies in wait for us.

1. *Ce n'est pas l'homme qui boit le thé, mais le thé qui boit l'homme* is the title of André Maugé's translation of Guido Ceronetti's *Pensieri del Tè,* Milan: Adelphi Edizione, 1986.

Dual Principle
Single Principle
Antagonistic Principle

Everything is in the play of duality.

The duality of the Other, whose world skims past our own without ever touching us – as in that 'duel in the dark' in the Chinese Opera, in which the two bodies and their weapons swish by within a hair's breadth of each other, describing the symbolic space of the conflict with their actions and silent confrontation.

The duality of gaming, which has rules that seem to come from some other sphere, with nothing to justify them – just like chance, that eternal unjustified principle.

The duality of feminine and masculine – the self-evidence of the duel between them – each being that in which the other is destined to lose itself.

The duality of Good and Evil.

The most difficult thing is to think Evil, to hypothesize Evil. This has been done only by heretics: Manichaeans and Cathars, both groups envisioning an antagonistic coexistence of two equal and eternal cosmic principles, Good and Evil, at once inseparable and irreconcilable. Within this vision, duality is primary. It is the original form – as difficult to conceive as the hypothesis of Evil.

For the phantasm is always that of the One as principle, of the single principle presiding over beginning and end. The world is One, and must become so again. This is the utopia of philosophical reason. It is, in a sense, the integral of the world – its being and its identity. One can conceive of the One dividing, but only the better to re-form its unity, for this unity is the norm, and any vision in terms of duality is heretical.

The dual hypothesis must have been very potent to be persecuted as it has throughout its history. Since it disappeared – first from theology, then from the whole of modern philosophy – everything of the order of a principle of evil has become deeply unreal and marginal. Any idea of a final destination other than the Good has disappeared from the field of analysis. This has become the true *pensée unique*, and Evil in this world merely has a walk-on part, exiled in thought while it awaits eradication in fact. It seems, however, that its principle is intact, its radicality unassailable, and that it is – at least in our world – one step ahead.

The philosophers never ask: why Evil rather than Good? This is because they no more believe in the reality of Evil than do the theologians. Or rather, they do not believe in the duality of Good and Evil. They posit Evil only to absorb it into a final reconciliation, a dialectical synthesis. Evil is always unreal; it is always in the pay of Good – it is, fundamentally, allegorical. In the Manichaean view, on the other hand, Evil has its own destiny, arising only out of itself, eternally enigmatic. It is from Evil that the world and matter and all created things emerge. It is Good which appears allegorical in a world dominated by the categorical instance of Evil.

There is no negotiating with Evil, since it is simultaneously principle, motive force and end. And the acknowledgement of Evil is already part of Evil. But then, if Evil is the rule and Good the exception, if concrete salvation takes the form of an accelerated destruction, and if everything is settled once and for all, why argue over Good and Evil?

But things are not settled, and it is the modes in which Evil appears and shows through against a background of the universal hegemony of the Good that are thrilling. Which of the two is at the controls of the suicide engine?

In fact, Good and Evil are not opposed to each other. They are asymmetrical in essence. They do not arise out of the same movement, and are not of the same nature. There is between them a kind of antagonistic balance.

If they were merely distinct and opposed – so that a choice between them, on which our morality is founded, were possible – then there would be nothing to prevent each from becoming autonomous and developing on its own account. In this way the world would become homogeneous through Good or through Evil. And we do in fact seem to be doomed to this today: to the homogenization of the world through Good and the imprisonment of Evil in a *musée imaginaire*. Without this antagonistic balance, we would be at the mercy of the forces of Good. In this sense, Evil protects us from the worst-case scenario: the automatic proliferation of happiness, a fate similar in kind to the automatic proliferation of cells when the mechanism of their programmed death no longer functions.

We are traditionally sensitive to the threat which the 'forces of Evil' pose for the Good, whereas it is the threat posed by the forces of Good which is the fateful threat to the world of the future.

Things do not stop there, however, and the complicity between Good and Evil is stranger than this. For it is Evil which pushes Good (the accumulation of positive forces) to excess and de-regulation, and it is the proliferation of Good which releases the worst evils. Behind all our techniques for unconditionally achieving Good lurks the spectre of absolute Evil. 'Evil has become a determinant reality,' writes Jung.

In the abysses of Evil which make up humanity's past – plague, torture, war, famine and disease – Evil was nonetheless not a determinant reality. Access to a higher idea of humanity, to a contrary reality, was forbidden to it, and something, passing through the ocean of flames, remained intact. . . . Jung adds: 'A so-called good to which we succumb loses its ethical character' (a marvellous formula this: it is not to Evil that we have succumbed today, but to Good). And what is a Good without ethical character other than an aspect of the legislation of Evil? . . . Now, with radio, telephones and excellent hospitals, hot baths, religious tolerance, moderate laws, an absence of war (in the most powerful parts of the planet . . .), an inundation of amoral *Good*, unstintingly produced by the entity Evil, by the powers of darkness enthroned in power – a terrifying contemporary *innovation*. (Ceronetti, *Pensieri del Tè*)[1]

Only Evil and destruction in all its forms still have the splendour of transcendence. Since all the transcendent values have been absorbed by technology, Good has conquered immanence and has, in the process, surrendered transcendence to the forces of Evil.

The new technologies are right-thinking in themselves and represent not only rationality, but charity. Virtue can no longer compete with machines and means of transport. It can only, then, become diabolical and regain inspiration from Evil. As machines have come to embody the idea of Good, so destruction and the technology of destruction have acquired a metaphysical character. . . . Annihilation is, then, no longer a metaphor. (Ceronetti)

Good, which was in the past an ideal metaphor for the universal, has become an inexorable reality – the reality of the totalization of the world under the banner of technology. So it is Evil which now takes over all the potency of the metaphor.

1. In translating this passage, I have restored the italicization of Ceronetti's original and indicated where passages have been omitted by Baudrillard.

The denial of Evil is part of the homeopathic treatment of our world – the treatment of Good with Good. But Good destroys itself: the optimizing of systems takes them to the verge of dissolution. And so this homeopathic treatment of Good by Good becomes the treatment of Evil by Evil. Universality of Good, transparency of Evil.

And what if the world were only now beginning to the full extent – whose limits will always remain incalculable – to unfold its origins from a principle essentially opposed to that of Good, a principle of Evil? This great Tribulation manifests itself as an inexplicable war, of which historical wars have merely been vague exemplars. (Ceronetti)

Like biological laws, Evil is impossible to modify. It submits only to those who are useful to its ends – who are Evil and nothing but. Evil penetrates and is not penetrated. It knows and is not known. As for whether it is begotten or not, there is no answer. What remains is the stupor and indignation at its effects, when these suddenly become too obvious. 'The world is unifying – but it is doing so by Evil and for the purpose of Evil' (Ceronetti).

An even more immoral hypothesis: Good and Evil are reversible. Not only are they not opposed, they can change into each other, and the distinction between them is ultimately meaningless. Naturally, I am not talking here about the innocent age before any distinction between Good and Evil, but, in our world, about a confusion of Good and Evil, which is precisely the mark of Evil, just as the lack of a distinction between True and False is the mark of simulation.

This is the iceberg hypothesis: Good is just the part of Evil showing above the water, Evil the submerged part of Good (one-tenth/nine-tenths!). There is no break between them, just a water-line. Otherwise, they are secretly formed of a single substance, of a single mass which, on occasion, flips over. Good becomes

Evil, and Evil shows up on the surface. And when heat melts the iceberg, everything goes back to the liquid mass of the neither-Good-nor-Evil. To take account only of the part of the phenomenon above the water-line (Good) is to run the risk of a lethal collision with the dark, submerged part of reality (Evil), which is infinitely more massive. The adventure of the *Titanic* provides an illustration of this (no one ever discovered what became of the iceberg, the 'living' incarnation of Evil).

Good and Evil transfuse even in the depths of the human soul, and make a secret compromise there. Saul Bellow:

> You say that in all of nature only man hesitates to cause pain. . . .[2] But reluctance to cause pain coupled with the necessity to devour . . . a peculiar human trick is the result, which consists in admitting and denying evils at the same time. To have a human life and also an inhuman life. In fact, to have everything, to combine all elements with immense ingenuity and greed. To bite, to swallow. At the same time to pity your food. To have sentiment. At the same time to behave brutally. It has been suggested (and why not!) that reluctance to cause pain is actually an extreme form, a delicious form of sensuality, and that we increase the luxuries of pain by the injection of a moral pathos . . . . Nevertheless there are moral realities . . . as surely as there are molecular and atomic ones. However, it is necessary today to entertain the very worst possibilities openly. In fact we have no choice as to that. (*Herzog*)

We do not have a choice between Good and Evil, since they are merely the transfusion or transfiguration of each other, in the literal sense in which each takes on the figure or form of the other according to a curvature of the moral universe

---

2. The French translator renders 'cause pain' as 'faire le mal'.

identical to the curvature of non-Euclidean physical space. The irresistible tendency of Good to produce negative counter-effects is equalled only by the secret inclination of Evil ultimately to produce Good. The two compete for contradictory efficacy on a more or less long-term basis. Another reason why the choice is impossible is that Evil is not in any sense the opposite of Good, and seeing the one as the mirror-image of the other is an optical illusion. Only Good posits itself as such; Evil does not posit itself at all. Like the Nothing, of which it is the analogon, it is perfect because it is opposed to nothing. Good and Evil, like masculine and feminine, are asymmetric: they are not the mirrors, nor the complements, nor the opposites of each other. The relation between them might, rather, be described as ironic. One of the terms scoffs at the other and at its own positing. In all essentials, they are not comparable. This is where the weakness of all analysis in terms of 'difference' lies. Asymmetric terms do not leave room for a 'difference'. Evil is more than different, since it does not measure itself against the Good, and thus leaves us no choice.

A way had to be found out of this impossibility of defining Evil and positing it as such. That way out was found in the confusion of Evil, on the one hand, with evils in the sense of unfortunate occurrences – misfortune – on the other. Misfortune (poverty, violence, accidents, death) becomes the transcription into the real of the spiritual instance of Evil. The failure to confront it as 'dominant reality' in all its ambivalence, in its (happy or unhappy) fatedness, the inability to envisage Evil, leaves us grappling with misfortune as an alternative solution.

Misfortune is simpler. You can tackle it with charity and virtue, with knowledge or compassion. It is a tangible object which you can share. In misfortune, the victims are the victims; whereas in the sphere of Evil, it is much more difficult to distinguish them from the victimizers. And, above all, misfortune allows you, in fighting it, to give a concrete sense to Good and to doing Good (which itself lacks definition). In the face of misfortune, Good can at last materialize and show its paces – which it cannot do against Evil, which always sidles up on it wearing a mask.

Yet Evil, too, has a great deal of difficulty showing its paces. When it wants to manifest itself as such – through violence, crime, perversion and transgression – when it wants to square up to Good, it falls into the same trap and the same moral illusion. What a desperate superstition was Sade's, and how superstitious are all those undertakings which take Evil as their principle of action. It is virtually impossible to do Evil for its own sake. (Being unable to spread Evil, you can always spread misfortune – but the same optical illusion occurs here as when you 'spread happiness'.)

In the short term, you can have the illusion of choosing between Good and Evil, with reasonable hope of success. But this applies only to a millimetric space of time in which a moral judgement can be expressed. The continuation of the action, the point where it gets embroiled in complications, fizzles out or even negates itself, are beyond us. Time itself enwraps each action in the sign of its end. This is how it returns into the random play of the world, a movement interspersed with brief flashes of rationality.

But where, then, is our freedom? It is possible to exercise freedom within a certain 'window' – the window of a moral reality whose existence we have to recognize, as Saul Bellow puts it, in the same way as we have to recognize molecular and atomic realities. Just as a certain set of phenomena are governed by classical physics, and another reality (though is it still a reality?) belongs to the field of relativity and quantum physics, so there is a moral reality and order of judgement which obeys the precepts of classical metaphysics and the distinction between Good and Evil, and another mental (micro-)physics which is no longer of that same order at all: a universe of relativity and no distinction between Good and Evil, where the question of freedom does not even arise. Here again, is this a 'reality' or is the only 'reality' the one subject to moral judgement, and to the imperative which grounds this same reality principle – leaving us, in other words, with a perfectly tautological definition?

At any rate, the two universes do not obey the same laws – or, rather, the real alone obeys laws and conventional distinctions. That which exceeds the real no longer obeys laws, and the concepts of will, freedom and purpose no longer operate. We have, then, to invent in metaphysical space (the space of Good and Evil, True and False) the same 'immoral' leap as represented in physics by the theoretical leap into relativity and quantum physics.

The existence of Evil is not a mystery. Evil (of semblance, illusion, uncertainty) is self-evidently there as a basic formula of our mortal existence. The real, on the other hand, as we picture it to ourselves, with its causal determinations and its truth-effects, is an exceptional phenomenon – in fact, the only true mystery. And it is a mystery whose secret we shall certainly never penetrate, for in the eternal balance of Good and Evil we shall never know where priority lies: with Good, as all our culture would have us believe, or with Evil and its spiritual adventure?

The two are entangled like the interwoven letters of a monogram. And if we move unfailingly towards the Good on a linear path, we equally surely come to Evil along another curve.

The most likely hypothesis, however, is that of the triumph of the final solution, that of a systematic integration by a single principle, for which we would merely have to 'pay an all-inclusive price'. In this ontological night, everything would be available 'in a single package', with no regard for detail. As of now, our adherence to an integral, integrist concept of the world and society is already very far advanced. We are on course for the perfect crime, perpetrated by Good and in the name of Good, for the implacable perfection of a technical, artificial universe which will see the accomplishment of all our desires, of a world unified by the elimination of all anti-bodies. This is our negentropic phantasm of total information. That all matter should become energy and all energy information. That everything in language should signify. That all genes should be operational. That everything should achieve self-awareness, and so forth. Abolishing absence, emptiness, meaninglessness. The phantasm (right down to the atomic level) of a mass without interstices, without inner distance; a mass of such infinite density that it ends in gravitational collapse. A phantasm at the human level of the abolition of all negativity, so as to produce an ever denser human substance, totally interactive, totally intermingled. Gathering time into one point, space into one moment. Everything being full, saturated, exhaustive.

In this hypothesis, towards which a kind of blind compulsion directs us, we must conclude with Ceronetti that 'concrete salvation takes the form of an accelerated destruction', but that it is not Evil, but Good 'which is manifestly at the controls of the suicide engine'.

The other – dual – hypothesis raises the possibility which stands radically opposed to that of a unified world and a single principle. By definition, the One is One, and can only repeat itself to infinity. But by what strange combination, then, does life transform itself? Why would it choose to differentiate itself, metamorphose and die, rather than persevere in its being by irrepressible totalization? Why wouldn't any form whatever simply go on realizing itself to the point of delirium? Why wouldn't any thought be exacerbated to the point of madness? If you assume a single term at the outset, it is not clear what would interrupt its running on in perpetuity. So nothing starts out from a single principle, and duality is the rule. To take up an intuitive insight from mythology: in every human action, there are always two divinities doing battle; neither is defeated, and the game has no end.

If the world were not the inextricable manifestation of two opposing principles, we would not be caught between relative certainties and a radical uncertainty. We would have only absolute certainties. 'Incertitude does not exist (but are you sure?).'[3] This is the same dilemma confronted by Cioran: 'You have to choose', he said, 'between the real or illusion.' Either the world is wholly real, or it is wholly illusion. Any compromise between the two is weak thinking.

Similarly, you have to choose: either Heaven or Hell – there is no Purgatory. It is the single principle or duality – there is no compromise solution. Yet all contemporary thinking on otherness goes on under the banner of this 'dialectical' compromise, playing on the countless variants of a soft, altruistic, humanistic, pluralistic thought – in reality, a *trompe-l'œil* invocation of the Other. The fact is that there is radical alterity only in duality. Alterity cannot be grounded in a vague dialectic of the One and the Other, only in an irrevocable principle. Without this dual, antagonistic principle, you will only ever get a phantom alterity, the mirror-play of difference and a culture of difference in which the great idea of duality is lost. Hence the need for Evil and Hell. Otherwise, we are in Purgatory and salvation for all – the 'right to salvation'. But if no one is damned any longer, then no one is chosen. You cannot have the one without the other. And if everyone is virtually saved, then no one is, and salvation has no meaning. This is where we are heading – towards an economic cast of things: merit and grace as equivalents, and salvation for all. Now, God could not lend Himself to this banal exchange, from which His entire *raison d'être* has disappeared, He having become a mere general

---

3. Passage in quotation marks in English in the original.

equivalent. Why would He bother with the upkeep of an eternal punishment factory? And if everyone is saved, what would be in it for the elect, deprived as they would be of the spectacle of the damned and their torments? So we need an irrevocable presence of Evil and Hell. Moreover, this has to be laid down by absolutely final decree, so that there is no threat to this duality from some sort of final reconciliation. The theory of predestination has no other meaning than to render impossible the banal exchange of Good and Evil.

If the world is what has no double, this is because it is dual in itself – in the original version, so to speak. Only in the dubbed (doubled) version does it become unitary.

The existence of the visible world originates in a breaking of symmetry. Matter, life, and even thought are the products of a breaking of symmetry. Subject and object, masculine and feminine, are asymmetrical. And it is this asymmetry which gives rise to the reciprocal attraction between them. For two things to be regarded as equivalent, and to be exchanged, they have to be wrested from this reciprocal attraction. They must not be able to change into each other. Otherwise, you are back in Alice's garden or, in other words, in Wonderland, the land of endless transmutations. Transmutations of ideas, of words – in the shaft of wit, the witty use of language – of the human and the inhuman, of life and death, of one sex into the other and, finally, of Good and Evil, through all the convulsions of Moral Reason.

Every life plays in this way with death, every body with its anti-bodies, every particle with its anti-particle, each sex with the other, in a kind of internal duality which means that nothing – forms, meanings, or the mass of living matter – goes on to infinity.

It is when the unitary principle unfurls itself in all its violence that this balance of life and death is destroyed. Wherever a symmetry and a mirror-relation is re-created (between the world and its double, between subject and object), it is done at the cost of liquidating this fundamental duality. This is the price to be paid for a final solution — the solution of a unified reality, a universal synthesis overarched by a single principle.

Dissociated Society,
Parallel Society

However, things are not settled once and for all, for as our society becomes globalized and as we identify, willingly or otherwise, with this integral world, duality resurfaces in all the modalities of disorganization which haunt our systems. And this includes even the denial of our own bodies and our own mental organization, which we manifest in madness, vertigo, absence, disappearance.

It is not even a question of a return of the repressed (which is still a mechanistic interpretation of the play of forces). It is simply that all liberated energy releases an antagonistic energy, that every difference secretes an equal indifference, that every truth secretes an even greater uncertainty. The fact is that there is no exception to what is not in any sense an economic principle, but a symbolic rule, and that the economy of all systems breaks down on the failure to recognize this fundamental duality, which then asserts itself through all the forms of clandestinity, dissociation and general, catastrophic upheaval.

Every integrating, homogenizing society tends, beyond a certain critical threshold (and our societies are now well past this), towards dissociation. Homogenize and integrate as much as you like; separation will still occur. The exclusion and discrimination will even increase in proportion to the 'progress' of integration. You will never get beyond the antagonism of two principles. In our modern societies this gives rise to the resurgence of a parallel society, a parallel market, a parallel financial circuit, parallel ('alternative') medicine and morality, even parallel reality and truth.

Any regime of control and prohibition creates an irregular, clandestine, anomalous situation: a black market. Prohibition and its consequences, along the lines of the prohibition of alcohol in the 1930s, has become an automatic mechanism of – and, in a sense, second nature to – our system. There is the black market in employment – the black economy – which corresponds to a deregulation of the official market (there is even, now, a black market in unemployment, duplicating real unemployment), the black market in financial speculation, the black market in poverty (the kind which circulates outside official channels), the black market in sex (prostitution), the black market in information (the many clandestine networks and secret services), the black market in weapons (a state-sponsored black market, but no less secret for all that) and, of course, the art market, itself now a veritable black market representing a kind of state of emergency and panic in the aesthetic field. Last but not least, there is the black market in thought. The liberal-democratic atmosphere, absorbing virtually all ideological divergences, or giving free rein to all *trompe-l'œil* differences, amounts to a state of advanced prohibition of thought, which has no other choice than to go underground. A piece of good fortune this (thought is not yet part of human rights, though that will surely come). As for alterity, it no longer exists on the official market, where it has been killed off by conviviality. There then automatically arises a black market in alterity, and, as usual, this one is largely in the hands of traffickers: it consists of racism and all forms of exclusion. A contraband alterity, all the variants of which (including nationalism, sects, etc.) will increasingly gain in virulence in a desperately integrist, unificatory, homogenizing society. All socialization is doomed to develop (as crypto-legally as can be imagined) all the forms of black market. Monopoly structures (and any state is a monopoly, since it claims a monopoly in the political and social spheres) cannot but secrete a para-political society, a mafia of some sort, to control this form of generalized corruption. It is pure hypocrisy on the part of the political authorities to fight this mafia, since it is an emanation of those authorities themselves. And, in the unimaginable eventuality that the authorities managed to crush it, then all of civil society would have become a counter-society, and the state a useless function.

Everything – or, at least, most essential things – already takes place outside the official circuits. And there is something heartening about this. There is something *spirituel* in this double game, in this perversion which resists any normalization, in these occult structures which flout established authority, in this black market of the social. And, in any case, what hope would there be for a society that had purged itself of all clandestinity? In the end, the last word goes to Mandeville, for whom the social body operates only through its immorality and its vices – but that immorality cannot be acknowledged: it, too, is part of the black market in truth.

This is our modern, corrupt version of the 'accursed share', that dangerous, residual, surplus portion which archaic societies well knew how to manage by establishing a double circuit, a dual register of exchange: the useful and the sumptuary. It is for us that it has become 'accursed'. It is because we have universalized exchange in a single mode, and flouted this symbolic distinction, that whole swathes of our exchanges and social relations have fallen into the 'black economy', have gone underground, where they continue to lead an illegal existence in the same way as the pagan gods continued to lead a furtive, superstitious existence under Christianity. So our essential decision-making and power structures, our networks and capital, are settling into the orbit of secrecy, of speculation, of an illegality so commonplace that it is no longer illegal. And this is also, in a sense, the continuity of Evil, the continuity of a vital illusion, a vital corruption which one might believe to be inscribed in nature. But it is inscribed in thought, and it is because it is inscribed in thought that it cannot be eliminated in fact.

This thoroughgoing dissociation of all the forms of society amounts to a veritable silent insurrection. It provides an echo of those peoples exiled behind the mirrors by the victorious Emperor, destined in the future to be merely a reflection of their conqueror. But one day, says Borges, these subject peoples begin to look less and less like their masters. They end up breaking the mirrors and bursting forth into the empire, laying waste to it. So we see entire populations rebelling – albeit in some cases silently – against the principle of representation. For them, the exercise of that particular freedom has become enforced bit-part playing and a shabby hoax.

   This is a very deep rebellion, which goes to the heart of the political system. What interest does the modern individual have in being represented – the individual of the networks and the virtual, the multi-focal individual of the operational sphere? He does his business, and that is that. What does he care for transcendence? He lives very well in immanence and interaction. What does a political will mean to him, a collective will, that glimmer of sovereignty he delegated to the social organization? There is no longer any delegation of the will, or of desire. The screen of communication has smashed the mirror of representation. Now only statistical shadows circulate – on the opinion-poll screens. There is no social contract any longer: on the media screens, only the image-playback functions. The citizen's only symbolic capital is that of his disaffection and political poverty, that very poverty managed by our official representatives (that is the secret of their corruption).

★

The political insurrection of people who no longer want to be represented, the silent insurrection of things which no longer want to signify anything. The contract of signification – that kind of social contract between things and their signs – itself seems broken, like the political contract, with the result that we find it increasingly hard to represent the world to ourselves and decipher its meaning. Things themselves rebel against decipherment – or perhaps we no longer wish to decipher them? It is the very imagining of meaning that is sick.

Yet we still play-act representation. A good illustration of this modern hoax was provided by the Kassel Documenta of 1997 with the 'Pigsty' Installation.[3] Reaching up on tiptoe to see over a fence, spectators look down on a pigsty, while a large mirror opposite allows them to see themselves observing the pigs. Then they walk round the shelter and park themselves behind the mirror, which turns out to be a two-way mirror through which they can once again see the pigs, but at the same time also see the spectators opposite looking at the pigs – spectators unaware, or at least pretending to be unaware, that they are being observed. This is the contemporary version of Velásquez's *Las Meninas*, and Michel Foucault's analysis of the classical age of representation.

Not only do people no longer want to be represented, they do not even want to be 'liberated'. Liberated from what, and in terms of what? For what is this liberty to be exchanged? What is exchanged in the system of representation? It is this impossibility of finding an actual equivalent for this freedom and this right to representation which constitutes the failure of the political today. Why bother to

1. The exhibit, a work by Carsten Höller and Rosemarie Trockel, was entitled 'Ein Haus für Schweine und Menschen' (A House for Pigs and People).

signify and assume meaning when everything circulates so quickly that nothing has time to be exchanged as value? To want what people want today, they do not need to be free. To say what they have to say, they do not need to be represented. To be what they are, they no longer even need to recognize themselves as such.

Hence the growing, epidemic abstentionism (and not just in the electoral field – that is merely a symptom), the creeping indifference, the viral indifference, itself in the process of infecting the system and wiping its hard disk. All these things were present twenty or thirty years ago in the analysis of the silence of the masses as rejection of representation, as disavowal of political liberty. But in this frantic world, the final throes of the political system have a deathly slowness about them. So we live in a world which is no longer our own, but in which, in the most absolute ambiguity, we collude. Subjects prey to the ghosts of their existence and their freedom; insolvent subjects, for they owe a debt which cannot be settled (there is no longer anyone to redeem the debt, nor any cause for which to sacrifice their lives).

However, behind this transparency, behind this vertige of a virtual presence, behind this indifference, isn't everyone subject to a demand of another order: the demand to be what they are – no longer by default, by being assigned to be merely what they are, but by excess, transfiguring this loss of representation into a vertige of pure presence? At last the good fortune to be what you are without passing through representation! At last the good fortune to want what you want without passing through freedom! Indeed, to do these things you no longer have need of anyone. As Cioran has written: 'What a pity that to find God you have to go via faith!'

Poetic Transference

Beyond Artificial Intelligence: Radicality of Thought

The hypothesis of a total identification of the world and thought in terms of a single principle is merely the most general one. The other hypothesis assumes a poetic reversal of the situation in which it is the very triumph of Good and the Single Principle which opens up the absolute singularity of the world and thought.

A radical re-evaluation: it is all these optimum-performance technical systems, these systems of limitless performance of the world, which paradoxically, in absorbing all information, in concentrating all functions in themselves, clear the way for the exercise of a thinking freed from all purpose, all 'objectivity', and restored to its radical uselessness.

If there is in our system a function which is in the process of becoming perfectly useless, thought must be that function.

Of the countless machinic prostheses with which we attempt to produce an artificial synthesis of all the possible activities of the human being, artificial intelligence (and computer technologies as a whole) is today the most prestigious and the most fraught with consequences. It is, truly, our chimera. For a long time now we have been living chimeras, strange mixtures of man and machine, and we have been living for some years in a chimerical cocktail of cultures, signs, differences and values – including that chimerical enterprise cloning, since in cloning we are coupled with our genetic doubles. But the finest chimerical assemblage remains the coupling of thought with its exact computer replica in artificial intelligence – playing with the demarcation line between the human and the inhuman in the order of thought, and representing a mockery of thought, just as genetic cloning represents a mockery of the species.

Soon, we shall no longer be able to think this mockery; it will have faded in the general indistinction of the computing sphere. Let us say, before it is too late, that artificial intelligence is incompatible with thought for the simple reason that thought is not an operation, that it is not exchangeable for anything whatever, and, most particularly, not for the objectivity of an operational calculation of the input–output type. For this reason, it cannot be taken over by any machine, or have any mechanical equivalent. It is out of despair at this situation that human beings have striven to embody it in a technical device. Perhaps thought is, ultimately, horrified by itself in its incompleteness, its ever unverifiable form, which is always irremediably complicit with a questioning and an illusion; perhaps it wants, in the end, to produce itself as function, fulfil itself as desire? In this sense, the entire edifice of information technology might be said to be the fulfilment of this perverse desire, aiming to efface itself before its virtual equivalent in the same way as the human species is aiming to efface itself before its genetic equivalent. And just as the coming of the clone is the final solution to the problem of sexuality and reproduction, so artificial intelligence represents the final solution to the problem of thought.

★

Fortunately, all kinds of things prevent that technical equivalence from coming about: feeling, perception, enjoyment, pain. Rest assured that efforts are being made to find computer-generated equivalents for all these, but for the moment there is still no machine to handle them.

What still distinguishes the functioning of human beings from that of machines – even the most 'intelligent' machines – is the intoxication of functioning, of living – pleasure. Inventing machines which feel pleasure is a task that is still beyond the powers of humanity. All kinds of aids can increase human pleasure, but human beings cannot invent any that would feel pleasure like themselves, or better than themselves – that would feel pleasure in their stead. They can make machines which move, work and calculate better than they do – but there is no technical extension of human pleasure, of the pleasure of being human. For that to occur, the machines would have to be able to invent human beings, or conceive of them. But it is too late for that. They can only be extensions of human beings – or destroy them. Machines would have to exceed what they are – to become metaphorical machines, parabolic machines, excessive machines. Now, even the most intelligent machines are nothing other than precisely what they are – except, perhaps, where some accident or breakdown occurs which you can always attribute to them as some obscure desire. They do not have that ironic surplus of functioning, that pain and suffering; they do not give in to narcissistic temptation, and are not even seduced by their own knowledge. Which perhaps explains their deep melancholy, the sadness of computers. All machines are bachelor machines. . . .

No doubt one day some will learn to give signs of pleasure, and of many other things, for simulation is within their powers. But they will just be imitating our psychological and social mechanisms, which are already engaged everywhere in multiplying the signs of desire, sex and pleasure – just as biological cloning merely plagiarizes our cultural mechanisms, which have long been doomed to mass reproduction.

Devices aimed at reproducing the complexity of the senses are already being cobbled together in the cybernetic interface. Touching each other 'virtually' at a distance. Using the subtlety of breathing, the rhythm of the pulsing of the heart, to navigate towards new virtual environments. Teleperformance, 'Very Nervous System', 'Telematic Dreaming'. The interface itself is a chimera, first in the Surrealistic coupling or grafting of man and his screen and then in those bioapparatuses – half-machine, half-organism – which 'will soon reconfigure our entire sensibilities'.

But what is ultimately going on here? Is the whole of the human undergoing a shift into the inhuman, or is the opposite taking place? Are human functions and reflexes being transferred into the machinic artefact, or are technologies being made subservient to reflexes that are human, all too human? Both are equally monstrous, since the human and the inhuman simultaneously lose their definitions in this intermingling. What is the point of this futile reduplication of our feelings, our taste, our touch and our mental operations if not to divest us of our natural intelligence?

If human beings create or fantasize about 'intelligent' machines, that is because they secretly despair of their intelligence or are crumbling under the weight of a monstrous, useless intelligence: so they somehow hive it off into machines, to be able to play with it, to mock at it. Leaving intelligence to machines is, in the end, relinquishing the responsibility of knowing, just as leaving it to politicians to govern us relieves us of the responsibility of power.

If human beings dream of original machines, machines of genius, that is because they despair of their own originality, or prefer to relinquish that originality and enjoy it indirectly through machines. For what these machines offer us is, first and foremost, the spectacle of thought; and human beings, in manipulating them, are indulging more in the spectacle of thought than in thought itself.

Not for nothing are these machines termed 'virtual',[1] since they keep thought in an indefinite state of suspense, a state linked to the achievement, at some point, of an exhaustive knowledge. The act of thinking is indefinitely deferred. The question of thought can no longer even be posed, any more than the question of freedom for future generations. So the men of Artificial Intelligence will move motionless across their mental space, hooked up to their computers. Virtual Man will be physically and mentally disabled. This is the price he will pay for being operational.

The confrontation between Kasparov and *Deep Blue* (and subsequently with *Deeper Blue*), between a human being and an 'intelligent' artefact, is a fine example of the hesitant first steps of the human being grappling with his immaterial machines, grappling with the mastery of his own intelligence, and dreaming of being that player who is greater than the game itself.

Man dreams for all he is worth of inventing a machine more powerful than himself, while he is nevertheless unable to envisage losing control of his creations. Just like God. Could God create a being which would outstrip Him? Yet this is what we are doing with our cybernetic creatures. We offer them a chance to beat us – and even dream of their outdoing us. Man is caught up, then, in a utopian phantasy of creating an artefact which is superior to him, but which he must none the less beat to save face.

1. The French adjective 'virtuel' has the sense of 'possible' or 'potential'.

If Kasparov initially defeated *Deep Blue*, that was because he still had a secret weapon – the weapon of intuition, emotion, the stratagem, playing a 'double game' – whereas *Deep Blue* had only powers of calculation. In fact, Kasparov is the only player here; *Deep Blue* is simply an operator. The automat never plays (except where there is a man hidden inside, as in Van Klemperen's chess player). Moreover, Kasparov has on his side the human passion of the challenge; he has an other ranged against him, an opponent. Strictly speaking, *Deep Blue* has no adversary; it moves within the scope of its own programme. This is a decisive advantage for the human, the advantage of otherness, which is the subtle precondition for play, with its possibilities of decoying, of 'overplaying one's hand', of sacrifice and weakness. The computer, by contrast, is condemned to play at the height of its capabilities. In short, in the human being calculation goes hand in hand with an ironic power, the ironic power of thought, a power which exceeds 'intelligence'. It is through thought that man can subtly de-programme himself and become 'technologically incorrect' to retain control of the game. But this situation is unstable: the day the language of the computer and the power of calculation come to prevail, the day man seeks to take on the machine on its own ground by becoming 'technologically correct', he will be defeated once and for all. And after the first game, we saw Kasparov moving in that direction: engaging in a battle of calculations and, in a way, losing his sense of the essence of the game.

By contrast, his opponents (the technicians programming *Deeper Blue*) got wise to this and worked on the interface, inculcating in the computer the real idea of play, and making the machine play against its own calculating nature by integrating human reflexes into it, and thus snaring Kasparov in his own trap.

Something incredible happened. Before the end, *Deeper Blue* rejected a move all the computers would have made and preferred a deeper one which did not bring it any great advantage. It was a subtle choice. And then later, in a winning position, it made a crude error, allowing perpetual check. How could it play like a champion and, only a few moves later, make such a blunder? It's strange. . . .

The IBM technicians had managed to inculcate a mental photocopy of the human into *Deep Blue*, in order to equip it to beat human beings on their own ground. By contrast, professional players dream of beating the machine as such, by becoming more of a machine than the machine. In this challenge, man is likely to be first to be knocked off his stroke.

The fact that the computer has managed artificially to synthesize certain human qualities does not, however, mean that it has begun thinking. It is merely being signed up to the technocratic project of reinscribing all data in a three-dimensional virtual reality. There is nothing new in this: we have already seen the successful rehumanization of industrial work within Taylorism, without anything of the nature of exploitation being changed. The inhuman can mimic the human to perfection, without ceasing to be inhuman.

Here everything rests on the distinction between intelligence and thought. The postulate, which was Turing's idea from the outset, is that intelligence can be separated from any physical substrate, from any sensible referent. Intelligence is not the intelligence of the whole human being, but a functional, cerebral version of ideation, and through it you can liberate an ideality of the human being restricted to the brain alone. Making a radical break between calculation and the body and, on that basis, inventing for yourself a definitive, spectral body, an exoteric body, free of any fleshly, sexual uncertainty, a body without depth, reinvented from the screen as skin, as tactile film, far removed from any organic sensibility. This is the perspective of the immaterial machine.

This ideality is, in fact, a delusion. The user invests the machine as another kind of esoteric body (his indefatigable exploration of the Net is equivalent to looking into his own body). It is not just the intellectual faculties but the whole of the repressed libido and the denial of the body which find their extension in the computer, which has become a desireless object of desire (perhaps this explains its emotional responses, its faults, its accidents, its viruses), while the human being becomes an inhuman outgrowth of the machinic faculties. In the interface, both exchange their negative characteristics. So the machine is just as much a victim of man as man is of the machine. Preoccupied as we are with the subject's point of view, we never envisage the possible alienation of the technical object, the danger of damaging or impairing it by projecting all-too-human fantasies on to it. The ultimate aim in artificial intelligence is for the machine no longer to seem like a machine, and to begin to 'think' – the machine must conceal its prodigious functional capacities to do as well (or as badly) as human beings. This is an error of judgement: preserving the specificity of man presupposes also that we preserve the specificity of machines.

However this may be, the use of computers does not simply bring with it increased calculating power; it modifies the types of phenomena susceptible of being processed. It becomes capable of bringing new phenomena into being, phenomena implied by a particular type of calculation. Computer simulation then becomes a form of interpretation guided by mathematical and technical models – a kind of new mental apparatus which does more than mirror the brain that designed it, since it analyses that brain in return, and shapes it in its own image.

If we opt for this type of intelligence – regarded as a higher function than all others, co-ordinating all others, but itself a function of a technical apparatus and operational models – if we confine ourselves to this high-efficiency definition, then the machine has got us beaten before we start. It is the same with thought: if it takes objective, rational truth as its aim, it is defeated before it even starts – by the experts, the logicians or the sophists.

It all depends on the ground we choose to fight on. Measuring his powers against a reductive ideal of intelligence, man is beaten by his own creation, his own shadow. This is, sadly, a very common model: most often – and this applies also to social and political matters – we choose to fight on ground where we are beaten before we begin.

We are forced, then, into a strategic redefinition of what is at stake in intelligence and thought respectively. And here Kasparov's defeat by *Deeper Blue* comes to our aid. Rather than fight on a ground where victory is never certain (that of technical intelligence), let us choose to fight on the terrain of thought, where the question of winning does not actually arise.

This is the key: maintaining the radical uselessness of thought, its negative predestination for any use or purpose whatsoever. In this sense, the threat posed by the development of artificial intelligence is a piece of good fortune. Thought is thereby rid of the burden of knowledge and information, of all the informational and communicational excess which encumbered it. The computer, which handles these things so much better, relieves us of all that. *Relieved of the real by the virtual itself*, thought can once again assume its place where 'the thinking is', where we are thought. For the subject who claims to think without being thought in return is merely an organic tool, prefiguring the inorganic intellection of the machine. He is beaten on his own ground, and in the end it is the virtual which thinks him. On the other hand, the person who thinks 'in return', the one who thinks because he *is thought*, is liberated from the unilateral 'service' of thought by the operation of the machine itself.

The immense advantage of artificial intelligence will have been to force thought into a corner: above and beyond the control of all its mechanisms, is there a particular purpose to thought? Is there something else within it which goes beyond its pure possibility of functioning? Does it still have an object once it has found its true object of perverse desire in artificial intelligence?

So we have to revise our judgement of this 'alienating' technology which our critical philosophy spends its whole time denouncing. And we see, rather, that we should extol the paradox by which all powers that arrogate ends and means to themselves also liberate those things which do not obey this functional principle. By arrogating to themselves a monopoly of meaning and knowledge, they liberate all those things with no meaning and no concern for meaning. Rendering unto utility that which is of the order of the useful, at the same time they render unto inutility that which is of the order of radical uselessness, and unto the void that which is of the order of emptiness.

Everything is much clearer.

Freed from all functionality (now devolved to the intellectual machines) and back underground, thought becomes free to lead nowhere, to be the triumphal effectuation of the Nothing, to revive the principle of Evil. And this turns everything around. For we said to ourselves, following Cioran ('What a pity that, in order to find God, you have to go via faith!'): what a pity that, in order to get to the world, you have to go via representation! What a pity that, in order to say things, you have to go via meaning! What a pity that, in order to know, you have to go via 'objective' knowledge! What a pity that, for something to be an event, it has to go through 'information'! What a pity that, for there to be exchange, you have to go through value!

Well, all that is over! From now on we are free with another kind of freedom.

Human beings, relieved of representation by their representatives themselves, are at last free to be what they are without going through anyone else – and not even through freedom or the right to be free. Relieved of value, things are free to circulate without passing through exchange and the abstraction of exchange. Words and language are free to correspond without passing through meaning. Just as sexuality, freed from reproduction, becomes free to deploy itself in the erotic, without a concern for ends and means.

This is how the poetic transference operates.

Where we might deplore the disappearance of the real in the virtual, the disappearance of the event in information, the disappearance of thought in artificial intelligence, the disappearance of values and ideologies in the globalization of trade, we should instead rejoice in this totalization of the world which, by purging everything of its functions and technical goals, makes room for the singularity of thought, the singularity of the event, the singularity of language, the singularity of the object and the image. In the end, it is the very existence of single-track thinking [*la pensée unique*], of the totalitarian system of the economy, of information and artificial intelligence – and the automation and exponential development of these things – which leaves space for a world that is *literally true*. It is the final accomplishment of reality which leaves room for the radical illusion. Now, it is in this literal truth, this literal play of the world, that the ultimate freedom lies.

Living Coin:
Singularity of the Phantasm

Pierre Klossowski's proposition, in *La Monnaie vivante*, of a phantasmatic transference (a variant of poetic transference) in which the economic becomes the place where singularity is embodied, fits in with this paradoxical perspective in which the system itself opens up a space for its absolute polar opposite. A perversion of the industrial order, a misappropriation of the abstraction of money for impulsional ends, and the paradox of a living coin defined as follows: 'And from this point on the industrial slavegirl substitutes for the function of money – being herself money, both the equivalent of wealth and wealth itself.'

Nothing less is involved here than the reinvesting of the sphere of all exchange by that which cannot possibly be exchanged. The phantasm, being unexchangeable, requires some variety of simulacrum before it can be traded. The economic sphere becomes this simulacrum. The sphere of value becomes the universally intelligible equivalent of that which is irreducible to value. What is at issue here is not a transgression of the law or of the economic order, but the perfusion at the very heart of that law and its abstraction of an impulsional element, an integral monstrosity. Without resolution or compromise: the monstrosity remains entire; only it transfuses through the abstraction which denies it. Something scoffs at exchange in the very sphere of exchange.

In a recent film, *Indecent Proposal*, a man (Robert Redford) offers to give a young couple a million dollars if he can spend a night with the wife (Demi Moore). What Redford would like for this exorbitant price is to buy this woman as-not-for-sale. This is not the price of prostitution, which would still be a commodity transaction, but the hyperbolic value of that which cannot possibly be exchanged, and the possession of which as such has no meaning. The appropriation of an individual human being has no more meaning than purchasing the words of a language for your own exclusive use. But what is not exchangeable in terms of abstract equivalence can circulate quite comfortably by elective affinity: words, property, women move easily from one person to another in seduction, without the intermediary of money, without the intermediary of meaning. Thus Redford could seduce Demi Moore and obtain the wealth concerned (the enjoyment of this individual woman) without the intermediary of the sign of wealth (the million dollars). But the challenge for him is precisely to take wealth by force *with* the sign of wealth: to prostitute not the venal part, but the unexchangeable part of this woman – her 'accursed portion', so to speak, the part which neither you nor anyone else can alienate from yourself, for the very good reason that it does not belong to you, that you do not belong to yourself. What one is, one does not have; and what one does not have, one cannot sell. Thus, even if they want to, neither can sacrifice this accursed share, even for a fantastic price. But the temptation is all the stronger to violate the inalienable form; to take by force, in its entrenchment, that which can give itself only in amorous collusion (Lacan: love is giving what you do not have – that is to say, what you are, which no one has at their disposal). Thus, genuine rape is not forcibly 'enjoying' someone, but forcing someone to have pleasure.

In the end, Demi Moore herself joins in and colludes in this profanation on the pretext of the couple's financial difficulties, though in reality she does so from a secret fascination – precisely the fascination with obliterating the very idea of impossible exchange (which is in some regard unbearable), with obliterating wealth in and through the sign of wealth. More potent than any other passion is this ironic, sadistic passion, this passion for total artifice, which is also the passionate desire to put an end to nature and to God's order.

In short, she agrees to spend the night with him for a million dollars. And it is on this basis of a cynical equivalence that they end up being seduced by each other – that is to say, each being deflected from their own principle to enter into a dual relation, to enter into wealth *through* the sign of wealth: and hence to bring about the paradoxical utopia of living money.

At the moment of fulfilling the contract, Demi Moore is still just a resigned victim, but she subsequently comes to life, revives as a woman. A decisive scene is the one in the casino when Redford asks her to bet for him at the gaming table – she gambles and wins. By this act, he seduces her. It is as though he were gambling the million dollars on her. As a result, she becomes the living stakes in the game, and it is as though she were taking the place of the million dollars he has given to spend the night with her. After gambling a million dollars, she puts herself in play for a million dollars. She no longer sells herself; she becomes the support or agent of an act of sumptuary exchange.

It is not that she 'is worth' a million dollars; as an individual human being, she is worth nothing. But the million dollars, gambled like this, is not worth anything either – and it is in this equivalence of non-value, in this equivalence of the nothing, that they can pass from the one to the other, from the one into the other, without losing in the exchange.

At this point, when she has gambled and won for him, she is 'lost', as they would say in *Les Liaisons dangereuses* (the best way to seduce is still to have someone do something in your stead: he or she will then keep on coming back to occupy that place). And indeed, *Les Liaisons dangereuses* offers a similar example: Madame de Merteuil has Cécile deflowered by Valmont to avenge herself on X, who wanted her to remain a virgin – and she makes this a condition of allowing him into her bed. In substance: if you take my place in vengeance, you will have your place in my bed. Little Cécile became the living coin of Madame de Merteuil's vengeance.

In both cases, the manoeuvre ends in failure. The difference is that in *Les Liaisons dangereuses* it ends in death (Valmont dies in a duel at the hand of Cécile's fiancé – she who served as living coin also has her revenge by proxy), whereas in the film it ends in the most mundane of ways: in a marital revival.

Once the moment of the transfiguration of money has passed, the moment of the reversibility of sign and thing – the million dollars metamorphosed into a unique woman, a unique sign – everything falls back into, and is lost in, a banal exchange of an amorous or sexual kind. The universal dream of negotiating bodies and pleasures above and beyond their value ends in speculation, inflation or deflation – in all the vicissitudes by which the economic order is usually beset. In fact, the paradox of living coin quite simply cannot be maintained. Except in the exceptional moment of this substitution, this transfusion of value.

The same paradox can operate not just in respect of wealth, but with regard to destitution, deprivation, mortification. Not only the realm of the impulses, but also the death drive has to find its living coin. A recent exhibition by the Spanish photographer David Nebreda illustrated an act of such self-denying bravado taken to extremes. Confined in a single room, seriously ill, he unflaggingly photographs his own torment, his own tormented body, varying the décor, the lighting and the staging of a dead-end world. At the end of a move more radical than any form of self-assertion, he finds the strength to inscribe himself in a living sign, the living equivalent of that mental destruction – the sign of his own body. His own body or his *personal* body?[1] At any rate, it is the only living object available to him in his reclusion with which to put his own death into circulation. So he gets himself on to another track, sets others off on another (false) trail – his own death is no longer an impossible exchange. He manages to deny himself absolutely and to produce that denial as work, and even as artwork. For his photos are not mere testimony, they are works. And this is where art appears as the perfect simulacrum: not just the sign, but the simultaneity of the thing and the sign. If one needs to say crucifixion, the sign which says it must itself be crucified. If one needs to say the life of the impulses, and find the living equivalent of the phantasm, the sign itself must be impulsional – that is, not in any way representative. Art is made from the impossible exchange of signifier and signified, and therefore from the impossibility of representation as such, which is made up of dead signs and empty promises.

Nebreda succeeded – for a moment. But the two things come together only ephemerally, and art, as the immediate incarnation of a living coin, lasts only for one dazzling moment. Most of the time, it sinks into trading on aesthetic values.

1. The French is 'Son propre corps, ou son corps propre?' 'Le corps propre' is one of the key concepts of Maurice Merleau-Ponty's *Phenomenology of Perception* (1945). The term locates the body not as something which we own (*our* bodies), but as a precondition for – and a means of – communicating with the world.

While I agree with Monika M. Langer that 'le corps propre' might be better translated in many contexts as 'the body itself' (*Merleau-Ponty's Phenomenology of Perception*, London: MacMillan, 1989, p. 39), I have retained the more common 'personal body' here, italicizing the 'personal', since I believe this formulation more accurately renders the distinction Baudrillard is making.

How do things stand today with all these strategies of singularity and the unexchangeable in the virtual space where, strictly speaking, neither signs nor money exist any longer? How do things stand with the drive and the phantasm, which have themselves become virtual or have, in other words, been substituted by signs which are no longer even simulacra, but computer-generated equivalents? For virtual reality is not a simulacrum. The digital, artificial language and the computer-generated image are not simulacra. In the virtual, the sign is no longer what it was, since there is no longer any 'real' for it to be the sign of. The era of the simulacrum was a golden age, the era of the drives was a golden age, the *empire des signes* was a golden age. This is the era of the digital, where the technologies of the virtual accomplish this miracle of abolishing both the thing and the sign – thus escaping their impossible exchange, but also escaping the *play* of their impossible exchange – that is to say, the invention and the becoming of living coin.

Commodity exchange, the abstraction of the commodity, of the general equivalent, and everything which describes the movement of value and the historic form of capital is one thing. The current situation, in which money is the object of a universal passion reaching far beyond value and commodity exchange, is quite another. This fetishism of money, before which all activities are equivalent, expresses the fact that none of these activities any longer has any distinct end-goal. Money then becomes the universal transcription of a world bereft of meaning. This fetish money, around which global speculation revolves – far above and beyond the reproduction of capital – has nothing to do with wealth or the production of wealth. It expresses the breakdown of meaning, the impossibility of exchanging the world for its meaning, and at the same time the need to transfigure that impossibility into a sign of some kind – indeed, of the most nondescript kind: the sign which will best express the meaninglessness of the world.

Does the world have to have a meaning, then? That is the real problem. If we could accept this meaninglessness of the world, then we could play with forms, appearances and our impulses, without worrying about their ultimate destination. If there were not this demand for the world to have meaning, there would be no reason to find a general equivalent for it in money. As Cioran says, we are not failures until we believe life has a meaning – and from that point on we are all fail-ures, because it hasn't. And it is, in fact, because this fetishized money is expressive of a pure and simple absence that it becomes speculative, exponential, itself doomed to crashes and sudden wild swings.

If you wanted to put a brake on the total extrapolation of the world into money, you would first have to eliminate the demand for meaning – that demand being increasingly thwarted, because the world has less and less meaning (it has never had any, it has never been exchangeable for anything whatever, but today it is increas-ingly difficult to find a substitute equivalent for it: the only equivalent we can find for it is a virtual one). We are thus torn between the imagining of meaning, the demand for truth, and the increasingly probable hypothesis that the world has no final truth, that it is a definitive illusion. Do we absolutely have to choose between meaning and non-meaning? But the point is precisely that we do not want to. The absence of meaning is no doubt intolerable, but it would be just as intolerable to see the world assume a definitive meaning. And this is where the miracle of money comes in. Money is what allows us not to choose between meaning and non-meaning, and so to find a universal compromise. It functions as a universal substitute finality, just as the fetish serves as a substitute sex object.

So, this money has no accountable equivalence; it is the universal equivalent of nothing – it might indeed be said, rather, to be the equivalent of the universal circu-lation of the Nothing. It is a disembodied sign, like the fetish object, which has nothing to do with the sexual act or pleasure. It is the opposite of living coin which, for its part, is the pure sign, the transfigured sign of impossible exchange. Money, for its part, is the sign-by-default of that impossible exchange – its fetishized sign. Become the absolute referent, it owes no account to anyone, and it will not be redeemed. In this respect it is similar to a debt, and it does indeed lead us into infinite debt.

There are two ways of breaking the law: to deny it or to be seized with a passion for it. This is, strictly, fetishism (and perversion in general): simultaneously possessing the law and the law's prohibition. In this we find the same paradox and the same challenge as in *La Monnaie vivante*: at one and the same time possessing wealth and the sign of wealth.

In Marx's analysis, the formal analysis of the commodity grounds a first-level fetishism, connected with exchange-value. But when the passion for value becomes embodied, beyond value, in the doubly abstract passion for money, this becomes the object of a higher fetishism, connected now not with exchange-value, but with the unexchangeable.

So initially, the real object becomes sign: this is the stage of simulation. But in a subsequent stage the sign becomes an object again, but not now a real object: an object much further removed from the real than the sign itself – an object off-camera, outside representation: a fetish. No longer an object to the power of the sign, but an object to the power of the object – a pure, unrepresentable, unexchangeable object – yet a nondescript one. An object of a 'nondescript singularity' (Agamben), like sexual fetishes which themselves become wholly objects of desire. One may talk about substitution and perversion here, but what is involved is an entirely different organization: a transmutation of the sign into an object, and hence a redoubled simulation, charged with a redoubled intensity. By this perilous leap into a double abstraction, the fetish becomes invulnerable: and here the subject is definitively protected from his object of desire.

Whatever the differences between commodity fetishism, sexual fetishism and the work of art, it does seem that this last partakes of the same strangeness, the same enigmatic, hieroglyphic character which Marx already attributed to the commodity in its abstraction and which Baudelaire transfers, by a double abstraction, on to the artwork as absolute commodity. Of all objects it is, in fact, the one furthest from the real world – the one to be taken as pure object, in its literalness, and hence as the object of an exceptional desire. As such, it is out of all proportion to the interpretation which can be given of it in the order of ideas, or even in the 'aesthetic' world.

This exceptional character can take any one of a variety of extreme forms. Fetishistic investment can run from the vilest thing to the most sublime, from the work of art to the most sordid of objects. Once one is beyond value and representation, the phantasm can find embodiment in any direction. In radical fetishism there is no longer any hierarchy of values, nor any history. The fetishized object escapes all difference, and becomes literal once again. It exists literally. It embodies the literalness of the phantasm.

This analysis of fetishism leads us towards singularity as itself an exceptional state of a raising to a higher power. Of the same order as the passage from simple simulation to the second power, that of fetishism. In the genesis of singularity there is, first of all, a passage from the general to the particular – but this is still relative to the general; then the passage to singularity as though towards a particular that is, in a sense, 'absolute' – henceforth unrelated to the horizon of the general. By this double perilous leap, singularity becomes its own horizon, its own event. It no longer has any definition or equivalent. It is reducible only to itself, rather like those integers which are divisible only by themselves. Singularity is a 'unique sign', as Klossowski says – and a sign without content. Singularities are, therefore, inexpressible by each other, and between them there can, therefore, be only a play of metamorphosis of the one into the other on the basis of *their non-existence as self-being [être-propre]*. Stripped of self-being, singularity therefore exceeds all our modern vision, novelistic or theoretical, which is a vision based on alienation and on the appropriation and disappropriation of self. Whereas the essential lies in the irremediable non-existence of the subject as self-being.

This is tantamount to saying that singularity *is evil*. It is that which it is impossible to exchange, the portion irreducible to any equivalent whatever. But by that very token it is the site of – and what is at stake in – integral becoming. This is how Nietzsche saw becoming: the possibility of an infinite metamorphosis on the basis of deposing both being and all those fictions presupposed by psychology and morality: 'There is no individual, there is no species, there is no identity.'

If the being in itself has its history, singularity has its becoming. And if history is bound up with an ultimate end, singularity, for its part, is bound up with the Eternal Return. History is merely the differential of change; the Eternal Return is the integral of becoming.

It is not a question of 'becoming what one is' – the point is that one becomes only what one is not, just as one *is* only what one *has* not. If singularity is bound up with becoming, that is because it is nothing in itself.

'*Bis Gottes Fehle hilft*,' Hölderlin tells us ('Until the absence of God comes to our aid'). God is the general equivalent in whose name everything changes and is exchanged. In the absence of God, everything can become freely, can metamorphose freely. In this sense, this whole business of living coin, radical fetishism and integral becoming is indeed a settling of accounts with God. For, if the very hypothesis of God has disappeared – if He is indeed dead, as Nietzsche said – we still have to deal – now, and for a long time to come – with His ghost and His metastases.

Real Event, Fated Event: Singularity of the Event

Media coverage is to the event what political economy is to the realm of the drives and the phantasm, according to Klossowski. Just as political economy is a gigantic machinery for manufacturing value, for manufacturing the signs of wealth, but not wealth itself, so the whole system of information and the media is a gigantic machine for producing the event as sign, as value exchangeable on the universal market of ideology, of the star system, of catastrophe, and so on – in short, for producing non-events. The abstraction of media coverage is the same as the abstraction of the economy: the information system supplies coded matter, deciphered in advance, negotiable in terms of models, just as the economy supplies only products negotiable in terms of price and value. And just as, thanks to this abstraction of value, all commodities are exchangeable one with another, so all events (or non-events) become exchangeable – if not, indeed, substitutable one for another – on the cultural market of information. The singularity of the event, that which is irreducible to its coded transcription and *mise-en-scène*, that which quite simply *makes it an event*, is lost. With this we enter the transhistorical or transpolitical realm – the realm where events no longer really take place, precisely by dint of their production and dissemination in 'real time'; where they disappear into the void of news and information (just as the economy disappears into the void of speculation). The sphere of information is like a space where, after emptying events of their substance, an artificial gravity is re-created, and they are put back into orbit in real time – where, having been devitalized historically, they are reprojected on to the transpolitical stage of information. If we see history as a film (which it has become, whether we like it or not), then the 'truth' of information consists in the post-synchronization, the dubbing and subtitling of the film of history.

We have, then, to get beyond the non-event of information to detect that which is resistant or refractory to it within its very process. To find, as it were, the 'living coin' of the event – to play on the way it is 'cashed in' in the sphere of information, as we do with the way the phantasm is 'cashed in' in the economic sphere. To make a literal analysis of the event, as one does of dreams, against all the staging procedures and batteries of commentary which merely neutralize it. Only events set free from the information system (and us with them) generate an enormous power of attraction. They alone are 'real', both unforeseeable and predestined, for though there may be nothing to explain them, everything in the imagination is ready to embrace them.

We have within us an immense desire for events. And an immense disappointment, as the content of the information media falls desperately short of the power of the means of dissemination. This disproportion creates a potential demand ready to pounce on any incident, to crystallize on any catastrophe, provided it matches up to this potential power which we don't know how to use (such disillusionment did not exist in a world limited, so to speak, to its natural boundaries).

And the immediate and universal emotional contagion which seizes the masses on some particular occasion (Diana, the Pope's visit, winning the World Cup) has no other cause. It isn't a matter of voyeurism, or letting off steam. Of course, people don't know what to do with their sadness or their enthusiasm; of course, they don't know what to do with what they are; but that is principally a spontaneous abreaction to an immoral situation. The excess of information creates an immoral situation in so far as it has no equivalent either in the real event or in our personal histories. So they feel the same resentment towards it as they feel towards the immorality of our societies, where nothing has any consequence any longer. Neither acts, speeches, crimes nor political events have any real consequences – a fact which finds expression in a spate of pointless trials (as for the Tribunal of History, that long since disappeared). Immunity, impunity, corruption, speculation and laundering – come what may, we are moving towards a limit state of zero responsibility (even the concept of a 'war with zero deaths' has something absurd and incomprehensible about it). Automatically, we want to see an event of maximum consequence, a 'fateful' event, to repair this scandalous non-equivalence with a sudden, exceptional responsibility. And this extends even to the case of a perfectly undeserved, sacrificial death (Diana). There is no element of death drive or sadistic ritual in this demand, no perversion of human nature. Neither the rational nor the irrational has anything to do with it. What is involved here is a symbolic rebalancing of the scales of destiny.

We dream of senseless events which free us from this tyranny of meaning, and from always being constrained to seek out the equivalence between effects and causes. We live in terror of both excess of meaning and total meaninglessness. Hence the hold which excessive events have on us, events which are to the banal context of social and personal life what the excess of signifier is to language in Lévi-Strauss's theory: namely, that which grounds it as symbolic function, beyond equivalences of meaning.

★

Getting beyond the 'real' event. Rereading it in terms of its ending, reading it as something predestined. Overturning the order of analysis, though not setting out to look for real causes, which can be accumulated *ad infinitum* without ever accounting for its prodigious effect. Explanation is always an alibi. The search for causes is always a denial of the event as such. It is the search for the conditions in which it might not have taken place. Now, the event which might not have taken place (the 'real' event) is much less interesting than the one which could not but have taken place (the 'fated' event).

For the same reason, the foreseeable event, which merely verifies the models and comes in at its predicted time, predigested by the information media, is less interesting than the one which rushes to an end, short-circuits its own causes and relegates them to a retrospective illusion. There is, in this way, a precession of the event, which always remains well ahead of the interpretation which attempts desperately to catch up with it, like sound chasing after objects which have passed through the sound barrier. In the time it takes to see it growing in our rear-view mirrors, it has already overtaken us. And when it is there before you, it is already too late. 'Events in this mirror may be closer than they appear.'

There are events which cannot but take place, and there are others which pretend to take place or stand in for something else. Any event can conceal another, and the violence which accompanies it changes nothing of the double game events play.

To decipher or decode an event is to analyse its relationship with its double: what can it be exchanged for? (and this will be its manifest meaning) – what can it not be exchanged for? (this will be its true meaning). Philip Roth writes of the taste for examining a particular social event in depth, as though it were 'a dream or a work of art'.

★

The dream of a total world of information has its opposite in a universe wholly made up of elective affinities and coincidences – not an accidental world, but a pre-destined one, since the coincidence is the opposite of the accident. In effect, what *can* not happen (if the probability is zero) in a sense *must* happen. It is one or the other: probable or certain. If it has no serious reasons not to happen, every event must succumb to the urgent necessity of occurring. All we can do is attempt to divert it – otherwise it will be fated to happen. And we know that every effort to ward off an event merely hastens its occurrence. We do not understand the force inherent in events that is their desire to occur. It is things not taking place that is the exception. All events will potentially take place: they are there *in potentia*. That *potentia*, that power of things longing to appear, is beyond our grasp. But it under-lies that sense of a priori certainty that something *must* happen.

If we think of all the causes, chains of events and coincidences which would have had to have been accumulated for that accident (the one at the Pont de l'Alma) to take place, it obviously never would have done (there is no point, then, in going back along that chain to explain anything whatsoever).

On the other hand, if we assess all that would have had not to have happened for the event not to take place, then quite clearly it could not but occur. There would have had to have been no Pont de l'Alma, and hence no Battle of the Alma. There would have had to have been no Mercedes, and hence no German car company whose founder had a daughter called Mercedes. No Dodi and no Ritz, nor all the wealth of the Arab princes and the historical rivalry with the British. The British Empire itself would have had to have been wiped from history. So everything combines, *a contrario* and *in absentia*, to demonstrate the urgent necessity of this death.

The event, therefore, is itself unreal, since it is made up of all that should not have taken place for it not to occur. And, as a result, thanks to all these negative probabilities, it produces an incalculable effect. Such are the lineaments of a Fate-based Analysis, an unrealist analysis of unreal events. And the death of Diana is an unreal event.

An unreal event, an immoral event. In the present case, the interminable commentaries on the 'accident of fate' or the 'fated conspiracy' merely betray collective remorse at being the virtual murderers of Diana – remorse linked to the secret sense of exhilaration, not so much at the death, as at the unpredictable event, the event 'from out of the blue', to which we are all so partial. In this sense, the pathos of the event is merely the expression of a – neither good nor bad, but quite simply immoral – collective will. And all the sentimental motivations invoked retrospectively are merely the moralization of an immoral event. All that merely masks the obscure object of our desire – namely, our desire for events, for an overturning of the order of things, whatever it may be; for a sacrifice of the most glorious figures (stars, politicians, etc.) – a perfectly sacrilegious desire for the irruption of Evil, for the restoration of a secret rule which, in a totally unjustified form (natural catastrophes are also like this), re-establishes something like a balance of forces between Good and Evil. All the tears and mourning reflect the fascination the automatic reversibility of Evil exerts on us.

And we are not passive spectators of this fatal episode, but full-blown actors in it, playing our part in a lethal interactivity for which the media provide the interface. It is said that Diana was a victim of the 'society of the spectacle' – she in the role of victim, and the masses in the role of ghoulish onlookers. In fact, what we have here is a collective scenario in which Diana herself is not innocent, but in which the masses play an immediate role via the media and the paparazzi, in what amounts to a positive 'reality show' of her public and private life – a life whose course they divert and the filming of which they consume in real time, in the press, on the airwaves and on the screens. The paparazzi themselves are merely the vehicles of this lethal interactivity (as, not so long ago, the Heysel hooligans, in moving from the role of spectators to that of participants, were the interactive operators of stadium violence). And behind the paparazzi there are the media, and behind the media, us. All of us: we whose desires shape the media; we who are the medium, the network and the conducting current. There are no longer either actors or spectators; all are immersed in the same reality, in the same revolving responsibility, in a single impersonal destiny which is merely the fulfilment of a collective desire.

Photography, or Light-Writing: Literalness of the Image

The miracle of the photograph, of that allegedly 'objective' image, is that through it the world shows itself to be radically non-objective. It is the photographer's objective lens which, paradoxically, reveals the non-objectivity of the world – which reveals that 'something' that will not be resolved either by analysis or resemblance. It is technology which takes us beyond resemblance, to the heart of the *trompe-l'œil* of reality. It is through both its non-realist play with technology and its *découpage*, its stillness, its silence, its phenomenological reduction of movement, that the photograph confirms its status as the purest, most artificial image.

The vision of technology is at once transformed. Technology becomes the site of a double game, the enlarging mirror of illusion and forms. Technical equipment and the world enter into collusion; 'objective' technology and the potency of the object converge. And the photographic art is now merely the art of slipping into such a collusion – not to control the process, but to play on it, and to show up as self-evident the idea that the die is not cast. 'Whereof one cannot speak, thereof one must be silent' – but you can be silent thereof with images.

★

Resisting noise, words, commotion with the silence of the photograph – resisting movement, flows, and ever greater speed with the stillness of the photograph – resisting the flood of communication and information with the secrecy of the photograph – resisting the moral imperative of meaning with the silence of signi-fication. Above all, resisting the automatic tide of images, their perpetual succession, in which it is not only the mark, the poignant detail of the object (the *punctum*),[1] which is lost, but also the moment of the photograph, which is immediately past and gone, irreversible and hence always nostalgic. This instantaneity is the very opposite of the simultaneity of real time. The flow of images produced in real time, which vanish in real time, is indifferent to this third dimension, which is that of the moment. The visual flow knows only change, and in that flow the image no longer even has the time to become an image. For an image to be of all things an image, it has to become so: this can happen only if the tumult of the world is temporarily halted, if there is a strategy of stripping things bare – if the triumphant epiphany of meaning is supplanted by the silent apophany of the object and its appearances.

Finding a literalness of the object, against meaning and the aesthetics of mean-ing – this is the subversive function of the image itself become literal: become, in other words, what it is deep down: the magical operator of reality's disappearance. The image expresses – materially, as it were – the absence of this reality, which 'only seems obvious and is only accepted so readily, because we sense that nothing is real' (Borges).

1. Roland Barthes speaks of 'marks' or 'points' which shoot out of a scene 'like an arrow'. This 'punctum' is 'that accident which pricks me (but also bruises me, is poignant to me)'. Barthes, *Camera Lucida*, London: Vintage, 1993, p. 27.

This is a phenomenology of absence which is usually impossible, because the object is normally occulted by the subject as it might be by an overintense source of light, and the literal function of the image is occulted by the ideological, aesthetic and political dimensions, and by the reference to other images. Most images speak. Indeed, they chatter on endlessly, drowning out the silent signification of their object. We have, then, to sweep away everything which interposes itself and gets in the way of this silent self-evidence. The photograph effects this disocculation by filtering out the subject, enabling the object to exert its magic, be it white or black.

At the same time, photography presupposes a technical asceticism of the gaze (via the photographic lens), which protects the object from aesthetic transfiguration – a certain nonchalance of the lens to bring out the cast of things, without forcing matters. The photographic gaze neither probes nor analyses a 'reality'; it settles 'literally' on the surface of things and illustrates their emergence in the form of fragments, for a very short spell of time – to be followed immediately by the moment of their disappearance.

Whatever the set-up, one thing is always present in photography: light. 'Photography': light-writing.

The light proper to the image. Not 'realistic' or 'naturalistic' light, nor artificial light either, but the light which is properly the imagination of the image, the very idea of the image. Not an emanation from a single light source, but, in a sense, from two sources: the dual sources of the object and the gaze. The image, says Plato, lies at the point of intersection between the light emanating from the object and the light from the eyes.

The kind of light we find in Hopper's work. Both the harsh, white, oceanic light of the coast and the unreal, airless, sterile light which arrives from some quite other shore. An irradiant light, which retains, even in colour, the potency of black and white. Characters, faces, landscapes projected into a light which is not theirs; lit up violently from outside. Like strange objects, illumined by a light asserting the imminence of a strange event. Isolated in an aura that is both extremely fluid and cruelly clear.

An absolute light – photographic in the literal sense – demanding not to be looked at but, rather, that we close our eyes to it and the inner darkness it enfolds. The same intuitive sense of light as in Vermeer, only there the secret is that of intimacy, whereas with Hopper it is the secret of an inexorable exteriority, a luminous materiality of things, of their immediate fulfilment, of an evidencing through emptiness.

This rough-and-ready phenomenology is a bit like a negative theology. It is 'apophatic', a term once used to describe an approach to a knowledge of God not by what He is but by what He is not. It is the same with our knowledge of the world and the object: showing it up through what is cut away[2] rather than in an open – and, in any case, impossible – confrontation. In the photograph, 'light-writing' is the medium of this ellipsis of meaning and this quasi-experimental decantation. (In the realm of theory, it is language which is the symbolic filter of thought.)

There is also – where this 'apophasis', this approach by way of emptiness, is concerned – a whole dramaturgy of the photograph, a dramaturgy of acting-out, which is a way of grasping the world by expelling it (acting it *out*), an exorcism of the world by the instantaneous fiction of its representation (and not by its representation itself, which always plays into reality's hands). The photographic image is not a representation; it is a fiction.

2. *En creux*. Compare *gravure en creux*: intaglio.

Perhaps it is the world itself which acts-out, which imposes its fiction. The photograph 'acts-out the world' and the world 'acts-out the photograph'. This gives rise to an almost material collusion between the world and ourselves, in so far as the world is never anything other than a continual acting-out.

.

In the photograph, you see nothing. The lens alone 'sees', but it is hidden. What the photographer captures, then, isn't the Other, but what remains of the Other when she or he isn't there. We are never in the real presence of the object (the Other). Between reality and its image, exchange is impossible. There is at best a figurative correlation. 'Pure' reality, if it exists, remains a question without an answer. And this is what these photographs are: a question to the Other which expects to remain unanswered.

In 'The Adventure of a Photographer', Italo Calvino writes:

> to catch Bice in the street when she didn't know he was watching her, to keep her within the range of hidden lenses, to photograph her not only without letting himself be seen but without seeing her, to surprise her as she was in the absence of his gaze, of any gaze. Not that he wanted to discover any particular thing. . . . It was an invisible Bice that he wanted to possess, a Bice absolutely alone, a Bice whose presence presupposed the absence of him and everyone else.'

Later, he photographs only the objects and walls in the studio, where Bice had been, but which no longer even signified her, and from which she had withdrawn for ever. But he, too, has also withdrawn. For we are continually speaking of the disappearance of the object in photography – that's how it was, it's not like that now – and there is indeed a kind of symbolic murder in the photographic act. But the object isn't the only thing that disappears; the subject also disappears on the other side of the lens. Every press on the shutter-release, which puts an end to the real presence of the object, also causes me to disappear as subject, and it's in this reciprocal disappearance that a transfusion between the two occurs. It isn't always a successful act, but when it is, this transfusion is the sole condition of success. It is, in a sense, an invocation – an invocation to the Other, the object, to emerge from this disappearance, and so create *a poetic situation of transference or a poetic transference of situation*. Perhaps in this reciprocity there is a glimmer of a solution to the problem of our notorious 'inability to communicate', to the problem of the non-response of the Other. And perhaps, too, there is a more subtle usage of indifference, and of the fact that people and things tend no longer to mean anything for each other. An anxiety-ridden situation which we try to ward off at all costs with forced signification.

Few images escape this forced signification. Few photographs are not short-circuited by being made to signify, to convey an idea of one sort or another – in particular, the ideas of information and testimony. Moral anthropology went down that route. The idea of humanity passed that way too. So, contemporary photography (and not just news photography) devotes itself to photographing victims as such, the dead as such, the poverty-stricken as such, yielded up to documentary evidence and imaginary compassion.

Most current photographs merely reflect the 'objective' misery of the human condition. Just as there is no primitive tribe which does not have its anthropologist, soon there won't be a homeless person amid his filth who doesn't find a photographer leaping out to capture him on film. Now, the more we are told about poverty and violence, and presented with them openly, the less effect they have on us. This is the law of the imaginary. The image has to affect us on its own account, to impose its specific illusion, its original language, for any content whatsoever to move us. For there to be an affective transference on to the real, we need the counter-transference of the image, and we need that counter-transference to be resolved.

We deplore the disappearance of the real, arguing that everything is now mediated by the image. But we forget that the image, too, disappears, overcome by reality. What is sacrificed in this operation is not so much the real as the image, which is dispossessed of its originality and doomed to a shameful complicity. Rather than lament the loss of a reality surrendered to the superficiality of the image, we should lament the loss of an image surrendered to the expression of the real. It is only by freeing the image from the real that we shall restore its potency, and it is only by restoring to the image its specificity (its '*idiotie*', as Clément Rosset has it) that the real itself can recover its true image.

This so-called realist photography *does not capture what is but, rather, what should not be*: the reality of destitution. For preference, it photographs not what exists but what, from a moral, humanitarian viewpoint, should not exist – while making perfectly immoral aesthetic and commercial use of this misery. It is a photography which attests not so much to the real as to a profound disavowal of its object, and also a disavowal of the image, which is assigned to represent what does not wish to be represented, assigned to commit a 'rape of the real'. So, the cult of the image at all costs most often entails an unhappy destiny for the image, namely, the fate of imprisoning the real in its reality principle, whereas the point is *to free the real from its reality principle*. Instead of this, we have been inoculated with the realist virus of the image, and the retrovirus of the image-playback. Every time we are photographed, we spontaneously size up the photographer as he in turn takes stock of us. And 'savages', too, spontaneously adopt a pose. Everything strikes a pose in an imaginary reconciliation.

Now, the photographic event remains a confrontation between the object and the (objective) lens, with all the violence of that confrontation. The photographic act is a duel; that is to say, it is a challenge to the object and the object's defiance of that challenge. Where that confrontation is ignored, there can only be escape into technology or aesthetics – that is to say, into the most facile of solutions.

One finds oneself dreaming of the heroic age of photography, when it was still a *camera obscura*, not the transparent, interactive thing it has become.

As in Mike Disfarmer's photographs of Arkansas farmers from the 1940s and 1950s. What we find there are people of lowly origins, posing conscientiously, almost ceremoniously, and the lens doesn't attempt to surprise or understand them. There is no pursuit of 'naturalness', but no idea of what they should look like either ('what they look like as photographed'). They are what they are, and they do not smile. They are not self-pitying, and the image does not pity them either. Caught, as it were, at their simplest, absent for a moment – the moment of the photograph – from their lives and their misfortunes, raised from their misery to the tragic, impersonal figuration of their destinies.

The image reveals itself, then, for what it is: the exaltation of what it sees in its pure self-evidence, without intercession, concession or embellishment. What it reveals is not something moral or related to 'objective' conditions, but that which remains indecipherable within each one of us; it is not of the order of reality but of the evil genius of reality, happy or otherwise. It is that which is of the order of the inhuman within us, and bears no witness to anything.

The object, at any rate, is only ever an imaginary line, and the world an object both imminent and ungraspable. How far away is the world? What is the right focal length? Is the photograph a mirror in which this horizon of the object shows up in miniature? Or is it man who, in the convex mirror of his consciousness, distorts perspectives and blurs the exactness of the world? Like those rear-view mirrors on American cars which distort the view, but warn you kindly of the fact: 'Objects in this mirror may be closer than they appear.' But are they not also further away than they seem? Does the photographic image bring us closer to a so-called 'real' world, which is in fact infinitely distant from us? Or does it, rather, keep the world at a distance by creating an artificial depth of field, which protects us from the imminence of objects, and thus from the potential danger they represent?

The whole question of reality is in play here, the question of the degree of reality. It is not, perhaps, surprising that photography should have appeared as a technical medium in an age – the industrial era – when reality began to disappear. It may perhaps even have been the disappearance of the real which gave rise to this technical form, in which that disappearance found a way to turn itself into an image. We should look again at our simplistic causal accounts of the genesis of technology and the modern world. Perhaps it is not technology and the media which are at the origin of this much-vaunted disappearance of the real. On the contrary, all our technologies – fatal progeny that they are – doubtless arise from the progressive extenuation of reality.

Shadowing the World

No language can become total at the expense of all others. You cannot imagine there having been just a single language in the beginning, and the prospect of a single language in the future would be a real anthropological catastrophe, as would that of a single species, a single way of thinking, a single culture. It would be the death of language itself in so far as it differentiates us from animal expression (the same for each species).

There is a necessary relation between the fact that languages are multiple and singular and the fact that language never says (only) what it means. If there were only one language, words, too, would become univocal, with their meanings set on automatic pilot. There would not be the same play between them (in artificial languages there is quite simply no play at all). Language would merely be an appendage of a unified reality – the negative destiny of a human species itself unified. It would always arrive after the event, whereas for us it seems that it has always been there in its multiple singularity. Indeed, it seems to be far ahead of us, and turning back towards us to think us. There is something more in the singularity of a language, which is that, even if it has an origin and a history, it seems to reproduce itself as it is at every moment, and to reinvent itself automatically. This is why we experience language as a kind of predestination, and a kind of happy predestination at that.

The predestination of thought is like this too. World or thought – which of the two thinks the other? What is the relationship now between thought and the world, which it no longer reflects and no longer claims to represent?

Yet thought is destined for the world; they are destined for each other. Thought is, in fact, the world's *éminence grise*, the shadow which accompanies it and, in following it, provides it with a secret destination.

It does not seek to penetrate some mystery of the world, nor to discover its hidden aspect – it *is* that hidden aspect. It does not discover that the world has a double life – it *is* that double life, that parallel life. Merely by conforming to its slightest movements, thought strips the world of its meaning, and predestines it for ends other than the ones it sets itself. Merely by following in its tracks, thought shows that, behind its supposed ends, the world is going nowhere.

The act of thinking is an act of seduction which aims to deflect the world from its being and its meaning – at the risk of being itself seduced and led astray.

This is how theory proceeds with the systems it analyses. It does not seek to criticize them, or set limits for them in the real. It maximizes them, exacerbates them, by following their every movement; it seduces them by pushing them to the limit. The object of theory is to arrive at an account of the system which follows out its internal logic to its end, without adding anything, yet which, at the same time, totally inverts that system, revealing its hidden non-meaning, the Nothing which haunts it, that absence at the heart of the system, that shadow running alongside it. An account which is both a pure description of the system in terms of reality and a radical prescription of that same system – demonstrating that it excludes the real and, in the end, means nothing. To duplicate the world[1] is to respond to a world which signifies nothing with a theory which, for its part, looks like nothing on earth. Neither an empirical refutation of these systems (which, were it to be done, would be part of the same reality), nor a pure fiction unrelated to them, but, rather, both of these things at the same time. It is both the mirror of a world which is already at its extremes and the thing pushing the world towards those extremes – the identification of an implicit trend, and of the force precipitating it towards its end. It recognizes that there is nothing to be said of the world, that there is nothing this world can be exchanged for, while at the same time showing that this world cannot be as it is without this exchange with theory.

This is why writing can take itself to its logical extreme, knowing that at a certain point the world cannot but begin to resemble it. But writing is capable of going to this extreme only because it follows the immanent order of the world. It reduplicates the world, and the world does not exist without this reduplication. The world lacks nothing before being thought, but, thereafter, it can be explained only on that basis. It is something like that 'nothing' which theory simultaneously reveals and supplants, an absence it both makes visible and masks. One may say also that the world indeed lacks 'nothing', and that thought is the shadow cast by that Nothing on the surface of the real world (path of nihility[2]). Radical thought is at the violent intersection of meaning and non-meaning, of truth and non-truth, of the continuity of the world and the continuity of the nothing. It aspires to the status and power of illusion, restoring the non-veracity of facts, the non-signification of the world, and hunting down that nothing which runs beneath the apparent continuity of things.

1. *Doubler le monde* might also be rendered as 'dubbing the world'.
2. 'Path of nihility' in English in the original.

Thought as illusion, as seduction, is no doubt an imposture. But imposture (and language itself is one) is not the opposite of truth: it is a more subtle truth which enwraps the former in the sign of its parody and its erasure. Literally, it plays at the 'game of truth', the way seduction plays at the game of desire.

In the end, what is the point of thought, what is the point of theory? Between them and the world it is a relationship of 'the Other by itself' [*l'Autre par lui-même*[3]]: suspense and reversibility, an asymmetrical duel between the world and thought. Always bearing in mind the three basic theorems:

- The world was given to us as something enigmatic and unintelligible, and the task of thought is to make it, if possible, even more enigmatic and unintelligible.
- Since the world is evolving towards a frenzied state of affairs, we have to take a frenzied view of it.
- The player must never be bigger than the game itself, nor the theorist bigger than theory, nor theory bigger than the world itself.

3. Baudrillard published *L'Autre par lui-même: Habilitation* in 1985 (an American version of which appeared in 1988 as *The Ecstasy of Communication*). The title plays on the long-running 'Par lui-même' series of critical studies published by Éditions du Seuil.